Time Warrior

Time Warrior

Using the Total Cycle Time System to Boost Personal Competitiveness

By **Philip R. Thomas**

With **Kenneth R. Martin**

McGraw-Hill, Inc.

New York St. Louis San Francisco Auckland Bogotá
Caracas Lisbon London Madrid Mexico Milan
Montreal New Delhi Paris San Juan São Paulo
Singapore Sydney Tokyo Toronto

Library of Congress Cataloging-in-Publication Data

Thomas, Philip R.
    Time warrior : using Total Cycle Time System to boost personal
    competitiveness / Philip R. Thomas.
        p.   cm.
    Includes index.
    ISBN 0-07-064274-5
    1. Product life cycle. 2. Product management. 3. Competition.
    4. Time management. I. Title.
    HF5415.155.T49   1992
    658.5′6 – dc20   92-4638
                                                        CIP

Total Cycle Time, TCT, Cycles of Learning, Total Competitiveness
Management, TCM, and The Five I's Process are service marks of
Thomas Group, Inc.

Copyright © 1992 by Philip R. Thomas. All rights reserved.
Printed in the United States of America. Except as permitted under
the United States Copyright Act of 1976, no part of this publication
may be reproduced or distributed in any form or by any means, or
stored in a data base or retrieval system, without the prior written
permission of the publisher.

1 2 3 4 5 6 7 8 9 0   DOC/DOC   9 8 7 6 5 4 3 2

ISBN   0-07-064274-5

*The sponsoring editor for this book was James H. Bessent, Jr., the editing
supervisor was Alfred Bernardi, and the production supervisor was Suzanne W.
Babeuf. It was set in Baskerville by McGraw-Hill's Professional Book Group
composition unit.*

Printed and bound by R. R. Donnelley & Sons Company.

Contents

Time Warrior

Prologue: Your Time, My Mission, This Book

The Time Has Come

If you will pardon a cliché, the time of your life is all you have, period. It is a seldom-acknowledged fact that for the majority of us, our main outlet for self-expression is whatever job we hold. It's a mystery why Americans seem to need a dichotomy between work and "what really counts" for them. Most of us are not artists, nor should we be. So what reason is there not to try to make your mark through your job? Because so much of your time is spent on the job, you should obviously make every effort to ensure that, professionally speaking, you get the time of your life.

Achieving the time of your life in the workplace—having fun, taking pride in your work, making your time work for you—is a function of the type of company you work for. Your chances are about as good as your company is competitive, and they will last only as long as your company *stays* competitive. The price of complacency can be disaster.

There is a way for your business to get competitive and stay that way, and for you to have a more challenging, rewarding working environment. I'm sure that there is greater potential for both than you have imagined. If you accept the connection between your personal needs for a better life and your company's need to improve its performance, this book will show you the necessary hows and whys. If you have made that connection, you are in for some hard work, but the results may well provide you with the time of your life.

If your company is already making an organized effort to become more competitive, pitch in. If it's not, you ought to size up the situation, grab a little self-empowerment, and spread the word. But not until you've digested the next eight chapters. It won't take long. It *will* be time well spent.

Welcome to the New Business Order

As the pace of international business quickens, countless U.S. companies big and small are undertaking programs to improve their competitive position. For many, this constitutes an overdue realization that the old, familiar, comfortable ways of serving customers will not do and that a substantial revamping of processes and attitude is necessary. For others, improving competitive position is a timely and salutary acknowledgment that the future belongs not to the biggest but to the quickest. Rapid, precise response to customer needs is the key to success in the nineties. That is the crux of the United States' much-publicized competitiveness crisis, a crisis I liken to a war against time.

The purpose of this book is to dramatize the urgency of the time war and to point the way to victory. That winning approach is called *Total Cycle Time*. It is a comprehensive system with which companies perform at their best while making the most of their on-hand resources. Total Cycle Time works. In case after case, in every variety of business, I have seen company employees galvanized by this approach's promise and its results.

Total Cycle Time works because it is not a theory but a body of practical, *proven* measures. With those measures in place, individuals at all levels improve their personal job satisfaction, security, and their private lives as well. This book states the case for Total Cycle Time and provides instruction in its use on an individual basis.

Time Warrior is the third in a series of complementary works. The first, *Competitiveness through Total Cycle Time* (1990), was aimed at top management, for it is at that level that a company's resolve to win the time war must rest. My second book, *Getting Competitive* (1991), outlined the impact of Total Cycle Time at the middle-management level, for it is there that decisive implementation of the new method must occur. But the buck, of course, does not stop with managers. The greatest weapon for winning the time war is forged when managers, inspired by leaders at the top, are supported by an informed, *committed* work force. In other words, the support and contribution of individual employees is crucial to victory in any competitiveness program.

This book, *Time Warrior*, is addressed to those individuals. In it, I adapt proven techniques into a practical guidebook for personal improvement. I will also demonstrate that Total Cycle Time is as effective in enhancing home and leisure life as it is in the work place.

Time Warrior is not an ironclad, nuts-and-bolts, hands-on manual for decisive change, however. Nor is this book full of platitudes about the virtues of self-sacrifice and dedication to a company. The corporate facts of life dictate that, to flourish, Total Cycle Time must be embraced by the power structure. The degree of employee support can make or break a company's attempt at improving performance, but in the final analysis, the will and the wherewithal for Total Cycle Time must descend from the top.

Nonetheless, individuals in the ranks can help jump-start the process by improving their personal results. *Time Warrior* will show you how to set things in motion with a few exemplary steps and will familiarize you with the details of Total Cycle Time. Once you have taken those to heart, your approach to work and its rewards will never be the same, regardless of the mindset of higher-ups.

A few words are in order regarding one of the key features I've built into this book. You will find it liberally laced with Reality Checks, real-life examples from both the business and nonbusiness spheres. Most of these Reality Checks are based on war stories collected in the course of my group's consulting activities. They are not all from my own experiences. Many, you will find, are contributed by my partners and colleagues, whom I would like to thank for their help, and they demonstrate the wide array of challenges organizations face and of creative solutions available.

Many different companies and industries receive coverage in the Reality Checks. Some companies' stories offer a host of lessons with implications for the "time war." Each represents a dynamic change environment, with potential for further positive change. They all offer different lessons, but together represent a solid cross-section of the U.S. economy, from small businesses to service companies to manufacturing, from low-tech to high-tech.

In addition, I have attempted to offer examples from a number of job perspectives—purchasing managers, human resources people, engineers, shipping and receiving personnel, shop floor operatives of all descriptions, supervisors, inventory, white collar, blue collar, and on and on. In other words, there should be something of specific value here for just about anyone who works.

The book's title is intended to dramatize the fact that, whether you realize it or not, you and every other American are locked in a vital struggle to maintain our nation's markets and develop new ones. If you or your company revamp your thinking accordingly, you can look forward to a more interesting, satisfying career.

You will be victorious in this war if you increase your competitiveness. Practically speaking, there really is no alternative. With Total Cycle Time, you do not need to work harder or faster. You *do* need to eliminate the countless hurdles that block effective performance and reduce job satisfaction and security. And everyone from the top down needs to sharpen response to customer needs, get results in less time, and use resources more effectively. If we do so, the payoff for all will be more rewarding, more meaningful careers.

Take to heart the ideas and methods of Total Cycle Time. If your company is serious about performance improvement, this is the book you need to gain real understanding of the ways and means of competitiveness. If, on the other hand, your company is complacent about competitiveness, you owe it to yourself to get familiar with Total Cycle Time's principles, *and you haven't a moment to lose*. In either case, when you put the lessons of this book into practice, you will be doing yourself a major service and making a visible, positive, permanent difference in your work and home life.

1

The Time Frontier

Buddy, Can You Spare a Minute?

Time is *the* most precious commodity, something you can neither buy nor create. In today's world, time is also getting harder to come by. More and more goods and services are designed to provide quick results. Those that fulfill the promise are being snapped up by the millions who are determined to "buy" themselves a little precious time. Perhaps you yourself take advantage of the time value of such products and services as:

- Express car-rental services
- Product code scanning in the supermarket checkout line
- Faxing instead of mailing
- Overnight parcel delivery services
- One-hour eyeglasses
- Half-hour, 'round-the-clock news coverage on CNN
- Five-minute microwaved dinners
- Two-minute, drive-through car washes
- One-minute Polaroid color snapshots
- Instant ATM banking

You and the Time War

People on the go may be willing to pay to save time, but many also let it trickle through their fingers like water. Some do so knowingly, especially on the job, because they assume that making better use of time is a matter of speeding up, of working harder. Not so. There are ways of getting the results you want faster but without additional exertion. I guarantee it. The general misunderstanding of time and its uses is tragic for business because timely response to customers and to change is the very essence of being competitive. Meanwhile, the battle for competitiveness has become a worldwide struggle. Individuals and businesses who master the art of precise, rapid response to customer needs will win in tomorrow's business climate. Those individuals and businesses who do not will fail.

Time Warrior makes two basic points:

1. The surest pathway to professional satisfaction, job security, and promotability is to join the worldwide battle for competitiveness.
2. You can win that battle by exploiting the opportunities in short cycle time.

A Call to Arms

The title of this book was chosen to dramatize the seriousness of the competitiveness issue. In today's world, any and all companies must accomplish more and more in less and less time; that is the greatest challenge facing business. Whether you realize it or not, you and your company are part of a global scramble for economic survival. Only the most competitive companies—those who respond to customers promptly and deliver top-quality goods and services at competitive cost—will survive the shakeout.

The competitiveness race is, for all intents and purposes, a time war. Thus your career becomes that of a time warrior. The enemies in this war are not the Japanese, or big government, or recession, or inflation, or your biggest business rival. Your enemies are much closer to home. They are the work habits, red tape, self-deception, unnecessary procedures, over-long processes, and outmoded attitudes that keep you — and your employer — from performing more effectively.

Becoming a time warrior involves detecting and destroying those barriers and liberating yourself and your company so that you both perform competitively. The personal payoff for victory in this struggle is on-the-job challenge, variety, advancement, and security.

An Arsenal for Survival

Wars are won by people equipped with clear objectives, high morale, and effective weapons. The time war is no exception.

The key to survival in the 1990s is the proper use of time, the most wasted resource in U.S. industry. The system for doing so is a comprehensive business work ethic called Total Cycle Time. Total Cycle Time shows individuals how to predetermine their absolute best performance level and provides them with the know-how to reach that level without working harder or faster.

Total Cycle Time works. It is the cutting edge of personal and business competitiveness, and, at this point, there really are no substitutes for it. It is the ultimate weapon with which to compete effectively in today's world. Total Cycle Time permits you to approach tasks in terms of the time you need to complete each necessary cycle of activity in your job — regardless of what that activity is or how simple or difficult it is.

Although cycle times are critical to competitive performance, they vary enormously from worker to worker and company to company. The best keep them as short as possible and measure their performance accordingly. I am convinced, and hope to convince you, that a stimulating, competitive work environment and a Total Cycle Time environment are one and the same. If you work in such an organization, you can look forward to an interesting, rewarding, and meaningful career. If not, your professional future is in jeopardy.

Indoctrinating Yourself

Total Cycle Time requires you to embrace a tough mindset, and, quite frankly, you must take the initiative in gaining and sustaining that mindset. It requires a degree of self-discipline many of us wish we possessed but few of us truly get around to developing. This time, let's really make the change. Here's what you'll need:

1. *You* must appreciate the seriousness of the time war's impact upon your personal well-being and your company's survival.

2. *You* must realize that it is in your personal interest to promote better, more responsive performance on the part of yourself, your subordinates, your peers, your boss, and your entire company.

3. *You* must shorten the time it takes to perform every task in the workplace without adding extra effort or speeding up your pace.

4. *You* must learn from experience, exploiting any and every practical lesson to improve your know-how and performance.

5. *You* must find ways to identify the actions you perform on the job that add no value and eliminate them.

6. *You* must adopt for keeps a new mindset by which you seek out and eliminate the barriers to quicker, more responsive performance.

These are the methods of a time warrior. Kept sharp and properly used, they will see you through the competitiveness crisis and position you for a much more promising future.

Friend or Foe?

When confronted by the realities of the competitiveness war, many working people rally 'round the flag without properly identifying the enemy. Is it unfair competition? Economic ups and downs? Poor leadership? Most often, it's none of these. The real enemies are on-the-job procedures and processes that keep you and others from performing to potential. Consider your own job for a minute. You've probably noticed a place or two where management might help your task run more smoothly or pleasantly. All working people have pet peeves about their jobs, yet there is too much hesitation to take action, too much time lost and frustration endured waiting for higher-ups to see the light. Most people figure that they are not to blame for the problem. Maybe not, but this sort of appeasement mindset simply doesn't work anymore in today's world.

You should refuse to accept a system that frustrates your best efforts. You should refuse, likewise, to wait for somebody else to see the light. Because you could be a casualty in the time war, you must use the weapons this book provides to fix things, regardless of your place in the chain of command. Faulty, barrier-laden processes containing many non-value-added steps victimize board chairs, CEOs, middle managers, rank and file, and support staff alike. Accordingly, waiting for the boss to do something is passing the buck. The boss is not the enemy, not even if he or she is inept. Your company's internal barriers are the enemy.

Combat Engineering

Barriers

To take necessary action, you have to get very sharp at barrier removal: targeting and destroying the burdensome procedures, obsolete methods, non-value-added steps, and self-deceiving attitudes that block effective performance. The number of such barriers is amazing; virtually every cycle of activity within the typical company is loaded with such obstructions. Demolish them.

Barriers in your area of specialty are the easiest to detect and remove, for you are the world's foremost authority on what it takes to accomplish your particular set of tasks. Professionally speaking, everyone is an expert on his or her personal actions, and only that person can mobilize that specific knowledge to best effect.

But bigger, more sinister obstructions lurk within your company's overall business processes and systems that prevent you and many others from working contentedly and productively. Classic examples are marathon meetings, multiple sign-off requirements, tedious inspections, checkers checking on checkers, and overzealous data gathering. How many of those would *you* miss if they were to disappear?

Barriers are procedures or steps in a company's activity that use up time, attention, and resources but add no value to the final product or service. Your winning tactic in the war for competitiveness is blasting barriers. Doing so will work wonders for your on-the-job satisfaction and for your company's survivability.

Substitute Processes

As you get proficient in the tactics and weaponry of Total Cycle Time, you will also spot *substitute processes*: measures your company uses to cope with internal problems but which do not *eliminate* the problems. Because they constitute a conscious response of sorts, substitute processes divert attention away from the root causes of problems, which continue to go unfixed. Like all enemies of effective performance, these processes must go.

Reality Check _____

Subject Industry: Manufacturing

Situation: Recently my job took me to a huge manufacturing company, where I was astonished by an unusual practice I'd never seen before. Each manufacturing area was equipped with a golf cart. When I walked onto the floor, most of the drivers of these carts, seated at the ready, were aimlessly perusing newspapers. I asked what purpose the carts served and was told that they were "expediters." Whenever a section of the manufacturing line ran short of parts, a driver fired up his or her trusty golf cart, raced to the supply area, and returned with a cartload of the needed items. That way, the line could avoid stoppages.

Comments: Although the drivers and carts were idle about 95 percent of the time, they were presumed to be earning their keep because they kept the line moving. In this instance, management had devised an outlandishly clever way of combatting repeated parts shortages, but no one had ever attacked the defective system that was causing the shortages in the first place.

_____

Substitute processes are costly, pernicious barriers to competitive performance. They add no value, and they camouflage underlying barriers. A time warrior knows not to mistake substitute processes for solutions.

_____

Steps That Add Value; Steps That Don't

Value added is the acid test for any procedure or step in any business cycle of activity. If a step adds no value, it simply ought to go. Life is full of no-value steps on and off the job.

Consider a typical visit to your physician. Your appointment with the doctor is at noon, but you arrive early in case there's been a cancellation. No such luck. Noon comes and goes, and you're still in the waiting room leafing through out-of-date magazines. It is close to 1 p.m. before the receptionist calls your name. You are ushered into an examination chamber and left with the assurance — unconvincing — that "the doctor will see you in just a moment."

"Just a moment" turns out to be 15 minutes. At long last the doctor enters, listens to your complaint, asks a few questions, pokes here and there, and scribbles a prescription — all of which takes about five minutes — then wishes you well and heads for the door. You look at your watch: it is now 1:10 p.m.

Not counting your early arrival, your cycle time for "seeing the doctor" is 70 minutes, only five of which constitute value-added consultation. In other words, better than 90 percent of your time has been wasted in activity that contributed nothing to the process.

Now, here is how a mindset accustomed to cycle time thinking — my own, in this case — approaches the problem. When this happened to me, I was determined that once was enough. Figuring my physician to be more attentive to phone calls than to personal contacts and having once talked to him by long distance while on the road, I resorted to the phone even when I was in town, insisting that the doctor bill the call as an office visit. That arrangement has worked out well, because reading back issues of *Medical Age* is not my idea of a great way to spend an afternoon. The new process involves not a single valueless step, and I don't miss a minute of work or play.

Now examine the pet peeves of your job situation in the same light. What are you trying to accomplish, and how much of your activity adds no value? Everyone can find a few no-value steps, but I'll give you some hints to get you started:

- Almost 50 percent of review meetings add no value.
- Almost without exception, inspection steps add no value.
- Almost without exception, multiple signature requirements add no value.

Sound familiar? In most companies, meetings, sign-offs, and the like are sacred cows because management adopted them to serve some purpose or other. But the fact remains that they add little if any value, so why should they be tolerated? As a time warrior, you won't allow them.

Exchanging Your Mindset

Besides making a case for the Total Cycle Time mindset and demonstrating how your own job satisfaction is linked to it, this book explains how to exploit it to your advantage. Total Cycle Time is not theory. Nor is it a program. It is the product of personal experience and practical application in dozens of real-life situations. The world is full of books and consultants advocating this or that approach to improving productivity, or competitiveness, or product quality, or professional happiness, or whatever. Total Cycle Time, however, is a winning strategy, a *comprehensive working business ethic* that has evolved from years of on-the-spot application.

How Much Fun Are You Having?

Having a good time on the job is possible for millions of well-intentioned people. You may be one of them. If so, "having a good time" needs to be looked at in a broader sense than usual. In today's consumer society, the advertisers' cliché of "a good time" is primarily recreational: a bunch of jocks yukking it up at a pub, or the dazzling femme fatale knocking 'em dead at a party. Those are simplifications of reality, of course. It's widely known (and backed up by reams of academic studies) that over the long term, individual satisfaction requires a lot more than occasional dollops of recreational fun. Yet there still exists a general feeling that the *good* times are the *"off"* times, far from the rat race. But think of it. You spend a fourth of your life, a third of your waking hours, on the job. Why shouldn't the *best* times—the most challenging and psychologically rewarding ones—be work-related? They can be, provided a competitive environment is in place. If you shorten your work cycles, you can enjoy that kind of payback without having to work harder or faster.

Which is not to say that your private life won't improve too. It will. You'll even get more mileage out of leisure time by importing practices you pick up from Total Cycle Time. And your off hours will be more relaxed because the time you spend at work will not have wound you too tight.

You Have More Time Than You Think

A good time is any time that's interesting and stimulating, which basically means any time not being wasted. With practice, you can cram more interesting experience into moments most people write off as useless.

One of the biggest frustrations imaginable is sitting stalled in traffic, an experience we all undergo all too often. Not only are those jam-ups no fun to cope with, they can ruin your mood for hours afterward. There is usually no way to avoid the bumper-to-bumper trap, but those bad times can be turned around in a number of ways, listening to book or language tapes, dictating letters into a recorder, getting a few calls out of the way. (To a busy executive, cellular phones pay for themselves in frustration removal alone!) Thus can a daily aggravation be turned into a rewarding interlude because you're doing something productive with the time. You can now arrive at your destination stimulated by ideas you might never have been exposed to without the gridlock. Life is full of opportunities like that.

Getting There *Isn't* Half the Fun

The popular expression to the contrary, a good time is getting where the action is without delay. Do I sound like a workaholic? I'm not. I absolutely need pockets of diversion from my job, but I want to spend my off hours enjoying such diversion, not traveling to and from it. I assume other folks think the same way, which is why, after work, so many people settle for quick-and-easy living-room TV or a few beers at the corner bar.

My recreational passion is fishing. As part of my business, I've set up a CEO training center in Louisiana. There's a small lake about 50 yards from my office door, not by coincidence. On a wall next to the door hang a dozen fully rigged fishing rods. When the urge to go fishing strikes, I simply grab a rod, leave the office, and, in three minutes, I know if the fish are biting or not. It's interesting to watch how many participants in our workshops get hooked on fishing. When we need a break from the intense pace, we track down to the lake, get a line wet, catch a bass or two (we throw them back), and return to the task refreshed inside of 20 or 30 minutes. The point is not that you should live near a lake, but that by being selective within your options, you can enjoy instant, hassle-free diversions from your routine.

Decompression Time: If You Need It, Use It

But that's me. Not all of us are alike. Perhaps you're the sort who needs to decompress between work and leisure. If so, just accept the necessity of transition time, and let it work for you. For example, among the acquaintances I've made in years of TGI training is one busy executive who deliberately does nothing on the evening commuter train so she'll be acclimated to the leisurely pace of her home life by the time of her arrival.

Selective idleness is an acceptable way of exploiting time. It can even produce pockets of inspiration. For me, fishing serves that purpose. It's so relaxing and untaxing that my mind adopts an unconsciously reflective mode. Without even trying, I often get an insight I couldn't see for looking while at my desk. Thus, pockets of diversion and pockets of inspiration are often one and the same.

Your Time Is a Valuable Personal Resource

During the environmental controversy over McDonald's use of petrochemically based styrofoam packaging (which it has since abandoned), somebody said that, pollution aside, "American consumers ought to treat petroleum with more respect, because it's too hard to come by to waste on throw-away boxes." That's a good point. By the same token, people ought to treat time with even greater respect, because there are absolutely no substitutes. And time is often so easy to save. For example, the fax machine, photocopier, personal computer, and Federal Express have cut the necessary work time for this book by 70 percent compared to a decade ago. That means more fishing and better concentration on other business priorities.

Time Without Interruptions

You need blocks of working time for undistracted concentration. Reserving them is a matter of arranging your priorities so that you're not juggling two issues at once and arranging your schedule so that you're not interrupted. Decide when to do what and stick to it.

Reality Check _____

Subject: Bill Hommon

Situation: Bill Hommon got hooked on *Late Night with David Letterman*. The show's wackiness was the perfect antidote to pressure on the job. The trouble, of course, was that true to its title, the show kept Bill up until all hours. Honing his sense of humor was costing him too much sleep and blunting his concentration the next morning.

Conclusion: Bill, it turns out, had a $300 problem that went away the day he bought a VCR, taped *Letterman* while he slept, and reran the show early the next evening.

Much frustration at work comes from people's inability to block out time so their concentration is not interrupted. This is especially acute in the white-collar area, where an interruption can be as damaging as an equipment breakdown on a production line. Why more individuals and companies don't address this issue is altogether a mystery. From coast to coast, companies of every type bewail foreign competition, unfair trade practices, labor legislation, interest rates, and what have you for their failure to perform more effectively, while the opportunity to streamline processes and accelerate results lies right under their noses, unattended. Whose fault is that?

Barriers: Attack versus Appeasement

Think for a moment about the things that prevent you from being better able to organize your work time. Whatever their nature, those circumstances are barriers. You need to identify and eliminate them. Many people get around workplace barriers by taking their work home with them. A few are quite happy doing so. But these people are creating a substitute process, a pipeline around the clogged workplace. They may be content to swap leisure time for professional peace of mind, but the system stays clogged. The trick is to unclog the system, not devise ways around it. The payoffs are improved performance, a corresponding rise in job satisfaction, and off time that is your own. If accomplishing that looks difficult, it is a sign that your company has some major barrier removing to do.

Back to the Old Grind

For me, the best times are being on the job, because my specialty really interests me more than anything else. My work is my fun because I have won the time war.

Since almost no one covets my job, it's clear that I haven't stumbled into a glamorous occupation. No matter. Years of experience have taught me that with a few obvious exceptions, work can be fulfilling and rewarding no matter what you do, provided some individual care is taken in job selection and the barriers obstructing effective performance are attacked and destroyed. When that occurs, your company will be performing up to its full potential, and you will have a challenging work environment.

2

Getting What You Want from Work

What Do You Want from Your Job?

Because you spend so much of your life at work, it makes sense to fight to improve the quality of life in that area. It is also likely that improvements at work will significantly impact your overall sense of well-being. Rest assured that the opportunities exist. But before you enlist in time war and prepare your attack, you must be sure of what you want in the workplace.

In all my years in the work force, I have discovered that people at all levels have virtually the same needs and seek the same things in their work. Perhaps your own objectives coincide with the list that follows:

You Want Job Security. It is comforting to know that if you're there for the company, the company will be there for you and that, barring acts of God, there will always be a spot for you so long as you remain competent. This universal desire is a bit trickier than it looks. Americans have historically defined job security largely in terms of legal and contractual safeguards such as wage contracts and guaranteed benefits. Such safeguards, unfortunately, create the illusion that the individual is somehow immune to the company's competitive position. Far from it.

In the 1990s, the worldwide battle for competitiveness is provoking a major showdown for U.S. businesses. Your company is in a struggle for survival, and, make no mistake, the next few years will be absolutely crucial. The key to *real* job security is to improve your performance and thereby to safeguard your company's ability to stay in business.

There are all too many cases showing how the wrong definitions of job security wounded a company's competitiveness, and there is enough blame to go around for both management and labor. The classic examples are steel and automobiles, where labor pushed hard for generous wage and benefit contracts and management proved ready to purchase short-range peace while ducking the issue of its long-range consequences. Meanwhile, the issue of staying competitive got lost in the shuffle. You know the rest.

You Want to Do Something Useful and Positive. We all need the satisfaction of honestly endorsing our company's mission. We also like to think we're contributing to a greater good. A prerequisite for such satisfaction is aligning your personal goals with your company's mission. If you are unable to do so, your morale will be low and your performance will decline accordingly.

Reality Check _____

Subject: John Arrison, a young member of the planning staff

Subject Company: Bath Iron Works, one of the last profitable shipyards in the United States.

Situation: John was bright, able, energetic, and had a first-rate education, but he had no future at BIW. A few years ago, the company had built its last commercial vessel and since then had concentrated solely on ships for the U.S. Navy.

Conclusion: Devoting his life to making instruments of war offended John's personal moral standards, so, after a good deal of agonizing, he left the company for a job that paid less but squared with his conscience. For John at least, that was a sound decision.

You Want Competent, Decent Leadership. Most conscientious employees need to know they can rely on their superiors. No one wants to have to second-guess faulty decisions, cover for inattentive managers, or, worst of all, take the rap when the boss louses up.

Developing accurate, pertinent performance measurements for all personnel is obligatory in truly competitive companies. In a truly professional environment, a poor manager has nowhere to hide. If you're permanently saddled with an inattentive or incompetent boss, that is likely to be just the tip of the iceberg.

Total Cycle Time imposes performance measurements that are relevant and dispenses with those that aren't. Until that occurs, you might benefit from working out a customized performance agreement with your boss. Such an agreement amounts to a kind of contract and clarifies both of your expectations. Furthermore, if you meet or exceed the expressed criteria, you will almost certainly be ready to fill a larger role within the organization.

It's interesting to ask business people what measurements are used to judge their performance. About half really don't know. Those who do are often rated on the wrong things, which can have some disastrous personal and corporate consequences.

Reality Check _____

Subject Process: Order Entry
Situation: Betty was being measured on the number of orders she entered per day, regardless of how long the orders had been waiting. A quick analysis showed a very wide range of order entry times—from 1 day to 40 days!

Analysis: Knowing she was measured by the day, to keep up her day-to-day momentum this employee had developed the habit of putting tough orders on the bottom of the pile. Those became the 40-day orders. She could hardly be blamed for that tactic, but she eventually found herself in trouble with both the long-suffering customers and her boss. When the by-the-day measurement was dropped in favor of another system, the long delays disappeared.

You Want to Be Treated Fairly and with Dignity.   Management has historically tried to practice fairness, although matters of dignity have not always been given equal priority. The two issues, however, are inseparable. Given the relationship between managers and their subordinates, fair treatment depends largely on developing and sticking to the right performance measurements.

Companies equipped for survival rate their people according to how much they learn from experience, how they apply those lessons to simplify their tasks, and, as a result, how often they complete tasks correctly on the first try.

Because appropriate monetary compensation is often central to the issue of fairness, an effective solution is to implant a compensation system wherein employee earnings are related to performance.

Reality Check

Subject Company: B&B Electromatic, Norwood, Louisiana
Situation: A few years back, I acquired B&B Electromatic, a manufacturer of electric highway barrier gates. For years, B&B had been troubled by poor performance. Turning it around took some doing. The habits of company old-timers were firmly entrenched, most of the work force felt isolated from the decision-making process, and even occasional bonuses had failed to sustain morale.

Knowing that a Total Cycle Time effort would require enthusiastic support, the company instituted a monthly bonus plan that was tied to profits. Everyone at B&B was included. The bonuses were based on a point system, and each employee knew how many dollars per point he or she stood to earn as profitability improved.

Outcome: The change in company morale was speedy and substantial. From top to bottom, everyone quickly grasped the connection between improved performance—*everybody's* improved performance—and compensation. What could be fairer? And, once Total Cycle Time began to improve profitability, what could be more conducive to embracing the new culture?

You Want to Learn and Profit from Experience.   Everyone needs to be provided regularly with objective information to increase understanding of the tasks at hand, permit a comparison with past performance, and suggest ways to improve. Such feedback may be as simple as a suggestion that you should be more prompt or as elaborate as using sophisticated software to measure corporate effort against previous achievement. Because feedback serves both a professional and personal need, it is vital to job satisfaction. In addition to occasional signs of approval, all of us need to see a connection between our daily efforts and concrete results for the company. That is what imparts meaning to the daily grind.

Examining and exploiting the lessons of experience is one of the most potent yet unappreciated opportunities in U.S. business. Accordingly, benefiting from experience is also one of the most important components of Total Cycle Time. I call these opportunities Cycles of Learning, and my mission is to encourage workers at all levels to use the information feedback of those cycles systematically and creatively. It is a mystery why the power of Cycles of Learning has gone largely untapped until now. Ignoring this power is like throwing away money or declining a chance to make work interesting.

CYCLES OF LEARNING IMPROVE CUSTOMER SERVICE AND CUT CYCLE TIMES

Every business is made up of a series of interlocking cycles of activity which together produce the product or services promised to the customer. Whenever a cycle or subcycle is completed, its participants have a chance to analyze their performance, spot strengths and weaknesses, and apply the newfound knowledge to the next cycle. There are precise ways of analyzing and exploiting the lessons of experience. Every Cycle of Learning must include a feedback loop that gathers current information and compares it with past performance. Such a process will expose barriers to more effective performance. The net result is that work becomes more simplified, and the time needed to accomplish work goes down, dramatically so in many cases. The professional and psychological rewards are obvious.

Reality Check _____

Subject Company: Texas Instruments

Subject Industry: Microchips

Situation: In the late sixties, I managed a division of Texas Instruments' (TI's) vast microelectronics business. By implementing Cycles of Learning and exploiting feedback, the division I was heading was able to cut its manufacturing time from about 13 weeks to 10 days. Since the competition remained in the 13-week range, TI became master of that part of the business. That was mighty good for profits and did wonders for morale. Inside a year, my division was getting seven times more Cycles of Learning!

Outcome: Because so little time now elapsed between the beginning and the end of a cycle, everyone could see and enjoy the relationship between effort and results. And because each Cycle of Learning offered clues to even better performance, the team could continuously add to its advantage.

Reality Check ─────────────────────────────

Subject: Roger Corman, Producer/Director, Hollywood, California

Subject Industry: Movies

Situation: One of the more interesting examples of the power of Cycles of Learning occurred in the world of movie making. In the fifties, producer/director Roger Corman became legendary for his ability to crank out weirdly fascinating exploitation films on the thinnest of shoestrings within days, not months as was customary at the big Hollywood studios. Oblivious to the accepted, plodding methods of the establishment, Corman was determined to squeeze every lesson he could from every project. That proved easy with so many Cycles of Learning, inasmuch as only a few days elapsed between commencement and wrapup of each film's shooting.

One of Corman's repertory players, incidentally, was Jack Nicholson, who claims to have made huge professional strides thanks to the rapid feedback he got from working in those oddball quickies. While his performance was still fresh in his mind, Nicholson could study the final product to see what he was doing wrong, and make the right improvements.

───────────────────────────────

 Cycles of Learning offer spectacular opportunities to increase competitiveness and improve job satisfaction. They are an integral part of the Total Cycle Time ethic and are one of your most potent weapons in winning the time war.

───────────────────────────────

You Want to Be More Competitive with Your Peers. There are few things more gratifying than knowing you are performing as well as or better than your colleagues. Furthermore, doing so widens a person's options. You increase the likelihood of keeping the job you have and of being sought after should you opt for greener pastures.

Regardless of the job, *every employee deserves at least four personal Cycles of Learning a year* so that he or she can put the latest lessons of experience to work. Most companies provide performance reviews annually, but a year is too long to operate in the dark. Quarterly performance reviews give you the specific feedback you need to deal with problems in a timely fashion.

Reality Check _____

Subject Company: Texas Instruments

Situation: The cycle time reduction at Texas Instruments described above involved three shifts. The output of each was packaged and tested during the shift that followed. That arrangement afforded the chance to track each worker's performance, and, in accordance with the fast feedback of Cycles of Learning, the results are publicized daily. When, for example, the 50 members of the day shift arrived at work each morning, they found themselves rank-ordered on a posted list based on the data gathered during the previous night's activities. Each person knew instantly how his or her performance stacked up against everyone else's.

Outcome: The impact on peer competitiveness was phenomenal. People at the bottom obviously didn't want to stay there, so we would pull them off the line for a short remedial training session, after which their performance invariably skyrocketed. That led to competition between shifts, which of course boosted our overall showing. Morale improved along with performance. Once a month, the top-performing shift received an award—nothing elaborate, usually a decorated cake and a trophy that the winning supervisor could exhibit as long as his shift held the lead. Needless to say, competition between supervisors also shot up as a result.

You Want the Tools That Will Help You to Be Productive. This largely self-explanatory requirement dovetails with the items discussed above. Tools can range from paper clips to robots. In assessing equipment needs, good managers take their cues from seasoned employees. But managers have a hard time providing the right tools when their companies' business processes are too complicated or take too long. It is incumbent upon employees and managers at all levels to scrutinize each cycle of activity so that steps which add no value are eliminated. Otherwise, adding resources and training just perpetuates old, counterproductive steps.

I can attest to this from personal experience. Once, on a visit to a manufacturing company, I noticed that every worker's station on the line had been reequipped with outsized benches to permit the stockpiling of additional inventory. The company was already up to its ears in inventory. Storing more was the last thing it needed to do. Unable to see the inventory trap, however, management had invested in more storage space as a way to improve performance.

To make matters worse, as work in process moved from department to department within the company, each item was inspected as it left one area and inspected again immediately upon its arrival at the next. This effort was totally redundant and repetitious, yet corporate myopia had prompted a decision to automate the inspection system. Had the desired (and expensive) equipment gotten into place, the company's faulty business process would have been entrenched for keeps—a close call.

Proper workplace "tools" should include the creation of short-cycle-time feedback loops to quickly exploit Cycles of Learning. Such tools are decisive weapons in waging the time war.

You Want Any Necessary Training to Be Productive.   One reason this country has one of the highest employee turnover rates is that managers fail to clarify performance details for employees. People often depart because they are confused about their jobs, a condition which could be dramatically reduced through proper training. Because turnover is expensive and hampers a company's performance, proper training is a must. Your personal well-being requires that you and your peers receive the best training possible.

Although the importance of training is seldom overlooked, its execution is usually mediocre because programs are geared to the largest common denominator of employee needs. If such is the case in your work area, you would be well advised to offer any suggestions you can to your boss. The implications of employee turnover require that effective training be given high priority by any company that is serious about staying competitive. And since competitiveness is time-based, training must be accomplished rapidly.

Training has come a long way in the last decade, especially in the realm of computer-based techniques. There are now programs that can easily be customized to an individual's training requirements, cutting orientation time and enhancing the coverage of specifics.

Reality Check _____

Subject: Employee Turnover
Subject Company: *Fortune* 100 company
Situation: A *Fortune* 100 company recently called on my group to help them with an obscene turnover rate of 35 percent per year. We started by changing the training method to a computer-based curriculum in which trainees could interact with the material and immediately see the results of doing things right or wrong. As is always the case, they responded to the right feedback. Accordingly, training cycle times were significantly shortened, and the program's applicability on an individual level was multiplied.
Outcome: As a result, the company's turnover rate dropped to about 5 percent, a 7-to-1 reduction.

In time war, swiftness and skill, not numbers, will prevail. Get adequate training.

You Want Your Company's Output to Be of High Quality.
For a person to gain satisfaction from work involves the production of goods and services that are timely, durable, reliable, and that set the standard for your industry. No other
psychological payback can match pride in your product.

Over the past decade, competitive companies have embraced the credo that high quality should be an actively pur-
sued objective, not an occasional, random side-effect. In fact,
it has become a truism that good quality pays for itself in satisfied customers, repeat business, employee morale, and public relations. However tempting it may sometimes be to neglect the quality issue, shoddy products bring nothing but
trouble in today's competitive world.

Too many well-intentioned managers, however, believe
that a high-quality product can result only through processes
that are complicated, painstaking, and meticulously inspected. Such processes can occasionally result in fewer defects, but in general they are at cross purposes with high
quality, because they increase the number of steps and potential mishaps that can occur. Needless to say, good quality
is pointless if your cycle time is too long to satisfy your customers. In the real world, high quality is driven by streamlined, simplified processes in which Cycles of Learning exploit the advantages of shorter cycle times.

Reality Check _____

Subject Company: Texas Instruments
Situation: One of the major headaches microchip
manufacturers used to experience was low yields. The
chip-making process was so complicated that the entire
industry resigned itself to high defect rates as part of the cost
of doing business.
Outcome: Our cycle time efforts at TI yielded an interesting
fact: As my team removed production barriers, simplified the
process, cut cycle times, and utilized the feedback loops of
Cycles of Learning, yields went up as well. The waiting, the
multiple and redundant steps, and the extra handling that
causes defects were eliminated. Put another way, the chips

weren't on the line long enough for something to go wrong with them!

Every corporate quality improvement program should be associated with a plan to exploit Cycles of Learning, remove barriers, and slash cycle times.

You Want the Power to Make Decisions. In addition to the proper handling of your specific responsibilities, you would like at times to act in your company's best interest, even if it means bucking the establishment, without fearing the consequences. Every savvy worker knows that this is easier said than done, especially in companies that set rigid limits on employee responsibility. Whether you sit tight and play it safe or stick your neck out for the good of the cause, you're in for frustration, right? Would-be innovators are further hamstrung by peers who base their decisions on what the boss wants to hear. As they become more competitive, however, companies invariably recognize that individual initiative is *essential* to continued high performance.

If your environment is less than competitive, taking the initiative may look dangerous. In even the worst companies, however, bosses rate their people on the amount of value they add, so it is not usually risky to demonstrate initiative. In the final analysis, what wins is what works. Anyway, do you have a choice? The alternative is to settle for a job in which playing it safe becomes your way of life. What's the satisfaction in that? What's the future in it? Settling only perpetuates uncompetitive habits.

Many organizational shortcomings that are obvious to individuals in the ranks don't fit precisely within a manager's specific area of responsibility. Spotting them, therefore, isn't always easy at the managerial level, and fixing them can be even tougher. A creative approach in such cases is for senior management to create a temporary team of diverse people whose job it is to solve a particular problem. Characteristically, these cross-functional teams are made up not of top brass but people from the middle ranks who possess the requisite experience and skills. Cross-functional teams are a creative, nonthreatening form of empowerment when the time is right for action.

Reality Check _____

Subject: Cross-functional teams

Source: Bill Wield, TGI partner

Situation: Charged with solving the problem of late deliveries, a cross-functional team at a West Coast company made a historic improvement in the chain of command. The team concluded that the barrier was senior management but was reluctant to carry such embarrassing conclusions upstairs. Conventional wisdom in the company had it that top brass was separated from reality by a "concrete ceiling." The team agonized about the politics and possible consequences of its conclusions, but ultimately the team's director courageously decided to call a spade a spade.

Outcome: Here, in Wield's words, is management's response when given the news: "The initial response was denial and defensiveness. However, through careful orchestration, the realization came [to them] that 'we had engaged the enemy and they are us!' The company realized for the first time the power of the cross-functional team, and senior management chartered the cross-functional team to continue to identify and resolve the root causes. The first charter was to develop an effective measurement system.... Further, cross-functional teams were created to delve into the details of poor performance. The concrete floor and the concrete ceiling began to crumble.

"The director's courage to address the issue was of utmost importance. Without this breakthrough, future success could not have been made."

The Time Warrior Creed, or How It *Should* Be: A Dialogue on Competitiveness between Employer and Employed

On the battlefield of competitiveness, time warriors need aggressive, responsive leadership, from CEOs (time generals) through middle managers (unit commanders). What exactly do your company leaders want from you as an individual? And are you willing or able to provide it? After all, it's only fair to reverse focus and look at your situation from the boss's point of view. Experience teaches much about the way things should work from the top down. Here is a creed of competitive managerial expectations, along with the sort of responses a confirmed time warrior should be able to give. Bear in mind that such a manager understands that only the fittest companies will make it in today's business climate.

THE COMPETITIVE MANAGER: I expect my people to arrive punctually and work effectively until quitting time.

The time war requires a company to get up and run. If anyone straggles in, the effort gets off to a ragged, ineffective start. That won't do. Furthermore, although you are not expected to live and breathe your job or to voluntarily burn lots of midnight oil, you do need to be available for extra effort from time to time.

THE APPROPRIATE RESPONSE: I will give my company and boss a fair shake.

If the company is to compete successfully, you must be willing to work your appointed hours and spend your job time to the best of your ability. That means being punctual, seeking the most efficient ways to use time, and not permitting personal affairs to intrude.

A fair shake implies that you will not be called upon to work excessive hours or in capacities beyond your training. Competitive companies don't need to put their people in such positions.

THE COMPETITIVE MANAGER: I expect my people to be concentrating mentally on their jobs.

You should arrive at work focused on the job at hand. You were hired to apply your skills and brain power, and your employer is entitled to expect all you can give during the time you're at work.

THE APPROPRIATE RESPONSE: I will manage my time on the job more effectively.

It is up to you to set aside blocks of uninterrupted time in order to maximize concentration. It is also essential to reserve time in which to think about what you have learned and how to reapply your experience more effectively. Since random, spontaneous brainstorms are rare, your boss should understand that thinking time *is* working time.

It is also appropriate for you to compare notes on performance with your peers and to share any insights with them. Perhaps as a group you can commence guerilla warfare on barriers that affect everyone.

THE COMPETITIVE MANAGER: I will empower my people to spot, target, and reduce barriers to improved company performance—wherever they occur.

Even the best companies need to smooth and simplify their methods, so it is everyone's responsibility to make barrier removal a part of his or her personal employment creed. Breaking through obstructions and slashing cycle times must be permanent commitments, not occasional hazardous duty. To paraphrase H. Ross Perot: When you spot a snake, kill it! Don't wait for it to slither into someone else's area.

THE APPROPRIATE RESPONSE: I will kill snakes. I will make vigilance a part of my skill set.

When you see a way to remove a barrier, you either attack it or document it and bring it to the attention of responsible parties. In addition, you should cooperate with others who are assaulting barriers.

In return, you can rightfully expect that those who decline to kill snakes will be judged accordingly. Pest eradication ought to be part of your company's individual performance criteria.

THE COMPETITIVE MANAGER: I expect that my people may sometimes do things wrong the first time around but that they will do those things right from then on.

Learning from mistakes is one of the most powerful of educational devices. After that, the secret in a competitive company is high first-pass yield — doing things right on one try.

THE APPROPRIATE RESPONSE: I will learn from my mistakes. I will improve my first-pass yield.

To do this, you must be armed with the mechanisms for learning: Cycles of Learning with a formal feedback loop to analyze what's being done wrong and right. First-pass yield and Cycles of Learning go hand in hand. You should also seek a performance review every three months to provide you with a personal Cycle of Learning. Accordingly, you should be evaluated in terms of your cycle times and first-pass yield.

THE COMPETITIVE MANAGER: I expect my people to exceed their designated responsibilities on occasion.

Killing "varmints" is everybody's business. If an employee chooses to ignore a problem in her or his particular area, everyone else is not entitled to do likewise.

THE APPROPRIATE RESPONSE: I will try to see my job as part of an overall, continuous business process.

Time warriors do not ignore barriers simply because the barriers are not on their watch or are beyond their daily responsibilities. Doing so weakens the organization's overall competitiveness, which in turn reduces both job satisfaction *and* security.

THE COMPETITIVE MANAGER: I expect my people to add value.

Companies survive in proportion to how well they meet the demands of customers. All employees must function as a team to deliver that improved response to customers.

THE APPROPRIATE RESPONSE: I will add value.

Think Like a Manager

Notice in the dialogue above how the competitive atmosphere is charged with purpose and challenge on both sides of the managerial line. (If you've already got the makings of a time warrior, you probably are intrigued at the prospect of working in such an atmosphere!) Notice also that many of these managerial expectations require a broader view on your part than simply being good at your assigned task. In other words, in a competitive environment, you will become more than an expert in your job's subject matter. You are expected to bear in mind how your task integrates with the big picture, how it is part of a seamless process involving everyone else. Removing barriers and substitute processes big and small is everybody's business. In case it is not obvious: Companies that strictly enforce the limits of each worker's responsibility are not in a position to compete, for they cannot root out barriers that fall into the managerial cracks.

3
A Lifetime of Employment

Job Security: Illusions and Reality

Most everyone seems to accept in principle that his or her company should strive to be more competitive, but quite a few balk at the notion that their personal job satisfaction is directly related to corporate performance. That's like saying there's no personal gain from being on the winning side of a war, or no harm from being on the losing side. Whether or not you agree, it would behoove you to consider that key issue in more detail.

Is security close to the top of your professional wish list? Probably, for who would object to knowing that the future held no on-the-job reverses or bad surprises? Furthermore, if you felt fully secure, your company would also benefit because you'd be able to bring all your skills to bear on the job at hand rather than fretting about survival.

On the U.S. business scene, job security is in fact a feeling, not an ironclad guarantee. Security is a condition in which you perform effectively, satisfied with your working environment. It is a condition in which your company has a bright future, and, because you are yourself competitive, you have the additional option of moving to another job if you choose. Job security is *not* a matter that can be negotiated or legislated.

The notion that individuals can negotiate absolute job security is wishful thinking, and the concept of risk-free lifetime employment is a pipe dream. Some people's aspirations to lifetime employment are undoubtedly inspired by the historic struggle of the U.S. labor movement; others may stem from working conditions elsewhere in the world. You've probably heard of Japan's paternalistic system in which new employees in effect sign up with a company for life. You may also know that in other nations (France, for instance), it is virtually impossible to lay off a worker without including a year's severance pay. In such circumstances, companies are more committed to providing a permanent place for employees than is the case in the United States. As Eastern European nations emerge from the wreckage of their planned economies, one of their biggest problems is that the work force, having grown accustomed to guaranteed employment regardless of performance, simply does not know how to work competitively.

Here at home, trade unions have traditionally defined job security in terms of increased wages and protective, seniority-based employment guarantees that limit the prerogatives of management. To some extent, Congress has also assumed responsibility for job security by enacting employment regulations that extend the rights of working people. Nonetheless, the United States' changing economic climate makes it unlikely that its unions and legislators will make further inroads in that direction for years to come. Meanwhile, the side effect of these developments has been to perpetuate an adversarial relationship between labor and management.

Job security is one of the fruits of victory in the time war. Because uncompetitive companies will lose the time war, they cannot provide long-term job security.

Five Sources of Genuine Job Security

Security through Competitive Performance. When you read of trade unions seeking lifetime employment guarantees, you may wonder if union leadership is also asking itself what its rank and file might do to assist company competitiveness, growth, and profitability, which is the only foolproof way to long-term job security. And in such showdowns as rocked Eastern Airlines and the *New York Daily News*, whose interests were ultimately served? Certainly not those of the long-suffering customers. Does that sound like managerial propaganda? If so, bear in mind that all the promises and guarantees in the world are worth nothing if your company fails.

Like security, loyalty to the company and to oneself are entwined. But your loyalty need not be blind *or* unrequited. There is scant incentive to be faithful to an uncompetitive firm in which you can take no pride. Managers of such outfits who think they can buy loyalty through juicy wage and benefit packages are kidding themselves in more ways than one, and so are you if you settle for that.

A few parts of the world are notorious for their lack of employee loyalty, a case in point being California's Silicon Valley, where high-tech companies stand wall-to-wall by the hundreds. Skilled people there are often careerists. As soon as the grass looks greener down the street, they move. This game of professional musical chairs has hurt quite a few promising companies.

Reality Check _____

Subject: Fairchild Semiconductor
Situation: Back in the seventies, as a divisional manager at Fairchild Semiconductor in the Valley, I was asked for my résumé by one of my engineering managers. He and his team, he said, wanted to see if I was worth working for. Perplexed by this request, I quipped that perhaps he had better give me his résumé so I could decide whether I wanted to keep *him*. His response was unruffled: "My team and I will work with you *if we want to*, because we work for ourselves, not for any particular company. Or any particular person."
Analysis: What was missing in that engineer's life was a satisfying job environment. But he had presented me with a legitimate managerial challenge.

At Fairchild, after we had shortened the division's cycle time and started to outperform the competition, that engineering manager who had read me the riot act surprised himself by becoming loyal to the company.

In most of the working United States, instances like the one above are unusual because there are not so many options. Consequently, if you like where you are living (or if you just don't want to move), it is incumbent upon you to merge your interest with your company's. As many of you know, this can lead to considerable discomfort and something less than optimum performance—unless your company is truly competitive.

Security through Rapid Response and Cycles of Learning. If you work in an environment where desired results occur in half the accustomed time, you will probably want to stay put. Managers everywhere are coming to realize that time is an important issue to career-minded professionals. Motivated people—time warriors—know the time of their lives is finite, and they want to see the impact of their efforts as quickly as possible. And why not? That attitude is exactly what is needed to keep a company on its toes.

Security through Accurate Feedback. If you are receiving useful, frequent, ongoing feedback, your work becomes meaningful. When you can observe the effect of your effort, you will take an interest in further improving the process, and you achieve that result.

Security through Job Satisfaction. Put simply, if you get twice as much done, you will get twice the satisfaction. And believe it or not, you will be twice as loyal to the employer who provides that kind of productive environment. Incidentally, you will also be keeping good company. Firms with a reputation for short cycle times have no trouble recruiting first-rate employees.

In the time war, it's what companies do, not what they say, that provides job security.

To achieve absolute job security, you and your company must outperform your competitors.

Don't rely upon wage and benefit promises of job security unless you are a time warrior.

Job Satisfaction: Are You in the Right Place?

Chapter 1 laid out the generic desires of a typical U.S. employee. Now it is time to get specific about the conditions under which you work. A time warrior's basic training involves adopting the competitive mindset, a process that starts when you face the realities of your company life.

Do you belong where you are? How well do your *personal* plusses and minuses mesh with your company's? Ask yourself the following eight questions. They may seem a bit self-indulgent, but they're not if you're concerned about the time of your life. Make a note of how many of the following questions rate a genuine yes answer.

1. Is the Chemistry Right?   Let's face it, every job has an emotional component that is crucial to effective performance. Sometimes you can pick up good or bad vibrations on day one; sometimes it takes a little longer. But by the time you've been at work a few weeks, you should know if the place *feels* right.

Recently, I interviewed a job candidate whose credentials looked interesting. He held a doctorate from MIT, his track record seemed made to order, and, as I learned during the interview, his appearance was in every way presentable. But I passed this applicant by because the chemistry was wrong.

During the interview, in some indefinable manner, he managed to rub everyone who talked with him, the wrong way. The decision was easy to make under the circumstances.

If the chemistry doesn't work, it is a dirty trick for a manager to hire someone, no matter how convenient or appropriate the linkup may otherwise seem. It is likewise a dead end for you as a prospective employee to go against your instincts when such an offer is made to you or to stay in your job if you feel bad vibes.

2. Do You Approve of Your Company?   Remember how important it was for John Arrison in Chapter 2 to find a company whose product did not offend his personal moral code? If you and your company are similarly out of step, helping to improve corporate performance can deepen your own moral dilemma. The issue of ethical compatibility extends beyond the usefulness and quality of products to embrace everyday business practices as well. For real job satisfaction, the social attitudes implied or expressed in the workplace must be acceptable to you.

3. Are You Compensated Properly?   Before you reflexively say no, reflect a moment. Because you live in a high-pressure, consumer-oriented, buy-now-pay-later economy, you probably feel you need more money to achieve your proper standard of living. Or perhaps, like so many of us, you are living on credit and would like to get one step ahead. I remember well how impoverished I still felt when, having reached a salary level beyond the dreams of my beginning years, my appetite for more products and services eroded my increased earning power.

Almost all of us want more discretionary income, yet whenever I ask employees on a job site if they would swap a 10 percent wage reduction for a job that's more psychologically satisfying, an overwhelming majority say yes.

Not all these yesses, however, are offered in a spirit of adventure. Some people willing to swap money for satisfaction are just playing it safe, because they associate making more money with taking more risks. But it does not have to be one or the other. A competitive job environment often provides the opportunity to have your cake and eat it too.

Many competitive companies are adopting a compensation policy of base pay plus such incentives as monthly profit-based bonuses, stock options, and profit sharing. Challenge becomes an explicit part of such packages. Everyone participates and everyone can see how individual performance is tied to the company's future. As corporate profitability improves, each employee does better. If there is a slip, everyone feels it.

Besides providing a positive link between effort and results, such a system also sensitizes each employee to her or his personal impact on everyone's compensation. Accordingly, foot-draggers hear from coworkers in short order. The system also encourages people at every level to innovate and suggest pathways to improved company performance.

Incentive-based compensation on a frequent (preferably monthly) basis is a shot in the arm for companies that want to motivate workers but sense that automatic or formalized wage increments are too mechanical.

4. Does Your Job Offer Enough Variety? Here's another question that invites an off-the-top-of-your-head "I want more" response. I seldom meet anyone who will admit to being satisfied with on-the-job variety. Even those with a substantial mix of tasks are seldom content. It is typical to disdain such administrative pushups as attending meetings, filing letters, and writing reports. But most folks like meeting new people and traveling far and wide. That is perfectly normal, especially for Americans, who seem to get bored more easily than others with repetition.

Quicker response and shorter cycle times come into play in this context too. They let you keep your mind fresh by handling multiple assignments instead of bogging down in one long rut. In a competitive corporate setting, employees routinely handle two to four times the number of assignments without having to work at a faster pace. Those long, deep ruts disappear, and so do the same old faces day in and day out.

5. Do You Accept the Trade-off between Your Rights and Those of Your Employer?   Every company's rights should be extensive, including the rights to regulate smoking in the workplace, insist on punctuality, prescribe dress codes, and enforce a certain level of office etiquette. Obviously, that's not everyone's cup of tea. As an employee, you should feel comfortable enough with your company's constraints to concentrate productively on your task. Your performance and/or self-esteem should not suffer because of the need to conform to limits on smoking, grooming, noise levels, or whatever.

6. Does Your Boss Deserve Your Professional Respect? When you interviewed for your present position, chances are your boss evaluated you partly on the basis of how well you could adapt to the existing system. But getting competitive requires a change in operating habits. It is time that employees reversed the process to determine whether the boss might be a personal barrier to productive change and, by extension, to individual job satisfaction.

7. Is Your Skill Level Right for Your Job?   Everybody knows someone who suffered professional harm by taking a job that demanded too little. In many places, such a move is a long-term career trap. If you took such a job with the promise of quick advancement but you're stuck in a slot that doesn't challenge you, that speaks volumes about your company as a long-term option. If you took the job hoping somehow to find a challenge, ask yourself if the challenge would increase after some serious barrier removal.

8. Do You Have Enough Career Time Left to Enjoy a Better Working Environment?   Here is another dilemma related to qualifications. Older people often feel trapped by their years on the job because they assume they are over the hill or are too pricey for better positions. Yet there is a growing body of happy-ending stories of people who learned to live on less in exchange for different, more interesting jobs. Nor do all burned-out people have to tighten their financial belts to achieve higher job satisfaction. There is also ample documentation of longtime employees whose careers took a turn for the better when their companies became more competitive. A competitive organization does not shrink from hiring people who have been through the mill and have the scars to prove it. Such people are usually winners, and it's easier to hire winners than to train them.

If you're a seasoned worker who wants to stay where you are, your task will be to adopt the methods presented throughout this book and rally others to the cause. You have a special stake in ensuring your company's healthy survival.

Now, if you answered yes to at least *four* of the above eight questions, your chances of job satisfaction in your current position are good — provided your company is truly competitive. Is that in fact the case?

If your yesses numbered *three or less*, there is a problem in your workplace. Try to determine if it is you or your company.

Can Your Company Compete? Ask the Right Questions

As the manager-employee dialogue in Chapter 2 demonstrated, a competitive atmosphere generates real-world job security and satisfaction. How close is your company to providing that kind of atmosphere? Now that you have pinpointed some of the personal plusses and minuses of your job, you must take a hard look at your company's performance. See how many of the following 14 questions you can answer in the affirmative.

1. Are Your Company's Measurements Clear? General statements on corporate objectives and commitments don't mean much without objective measurements. You should be able to see a direct relationship between the way you are measured on your job and the overall measurements the company uses in its reports, press releases, and publications.

2. Is Your Company's Reputation One of High Integrity? Integrity, competitiveness, and job satisfaction are interlocked. For example, my mindset would make it impossible to work in a company that ignored the issue of rapid response or sold poor quality items to captive clients — unless I could do something to change such practices. Integrity also embraces changes in ethical values that have entered the workplace. Until lately, the business world abided racial prejudice, sexual harassment, liquid lunches, and unrestricted smoking as routine. It's clear those days are over. Healthy companies now require higher personal standards. Being competitive is partly a matter of enforcing the right criteria, and a company that tolerates Dark Age social attitudes is in trouble.

3. Does Your Company's Product Line Make Sense? This may be a tough question to answer without a lot of reflection. Presumably you're not being paid to make products for which there is no market. (If you are, you won't be at it long, so you should arrange your exit as soon as possible.) But it is by no means rare to encounter troubled firms that have failed to fine-tune their product strategy and are therefore misdirecting their efforts.

Reality Check _____

Subject: Philips/Signetics
Subject Industry: Microchip Manufacturing
Situation: Signetics is an important microchip manufacturer whose design, development, and manufacturing cycles were

ruinously long and whose monthly losses were high. Shortening those cycles made it possible for new products to reach the market in a more timely fashion, but that alone did not solve the profitability crisis. Signetics' biggest sellers were several loss leaders priced below a dollar. The company was therefore getting better and better at making the wrong items.

Outcome: It was discovered that the sought-after turnaround would therefore require complementing improvements in business processes by revamping the product line.

4. Are the Values and Traditions of Your Company Compatible with the Elements of Competitiveness?

Is there a conflict of principle between the accepted way your company does business and these three key indicators of competitiveness:

- Short cycle times
- Quicker response to customers
- Cycles of Learning

A frequent example of conflicting principles involves product quality. Nobody is against high quality, just as nobody is against motherhood or being more responsive to customers. The problem is not *whether* to upgrade quality but *how*. Too many companies try to improve quality by adding new, painstaking steps such as inspections instead of eliminating existing steps that are complicating work and increasing the chance of error. Long, complex cycle times are often taken as evidence that a company is careful. Eliminating them implies carelessness. Nothing could be further from the truth.

5. Does Your Company Operate with a Seamless Business Process?

In other words, from where you sit, can you perceive a clear, unified process embracing the entire corporate cycle of activity? Or are there major obstructions to a smooth process flow? If there are no minefields to cross in accomplishing your daily task, if no special efforts are necessary when you want to expedite work, and if your routine is not interrupted by periodic "hot-lots" or high-priority rush jobs, you are in good shape and can answer yes to this question.

6. Is Your Company Managed from Back to Front? A book such as this one is read from the front to the back; businesses should be run from the back to the front. Ideally, your company's business process should work back from what your customers need; all forecasting, planning, and manufacturing should be based upon that reality.

Reality Check _____

Subject: Federal Express
Subject Industry: Fast delivery
Situation: Federal Express is a good example of back-to-front management. The entire Fed Ex operation has been designed to satisfy customer needs: accurate, timely delivery with instant tracking of any misplaced packages and instant correction if something goes wrong.
Comment: Very few businesses are set up that way. Most operate from the middle outward: Managers consider their existing capability first and then try to bend market opportunity to fit it.

Reality Check _____

Subject: Publishing
Situation: I once visited a publishing company whose books sold regularly though not spectacularly but whose enormous presses could crank out lot sizes of more than a million. Fixated on that capability, the company habitually printed warehouse-size lots and put them into inventory, all in the name of optimizing the use of the equipment's capacity. Although there was an eventual market for all those books, apparently little thought had been given to the fact that customers' immediate needs were for smaller, assorted lots.
Analysis: Management had lost control of that company; the equipment had taken over. In this case, massive output had nothing to do with effective performance.

Back-to-front management has its priorities in order. Its top priority is to address the needs of its customers in timely, responsive fashion.

7. Is Your Company Known for Its Fast Response in the Marketplace?   If you can answer yes to this one, your outfit has mastered a critical step, and the word has probably gotten around. Or does the grapevine sing a different tune? Companies unable to get quotations to customers fast enough get plenty of negative feedback from hard-pressed field representatives. Companies unable to deliver within the customer's time frame simply lose their clientele.

8. Are You Largely Free from Rework in Your Area?   In other words, do you enjoy high first-pass yield? Excessive rework is a dead giveaway of an uncompetitive company, and nowhere is the problem so clear as down in the ranks. Upper management often overlooks rework in process when computing first-pass yield and gives itself unrealistically high grades in that department because the finished products are not defective. People in the lower ranks know better, because they are the ones who have had to rework those products to get them up to standard.

In most offices, for example, the secretary has the real dope on clerical rework, not the boss. The boss has no idea how many times a flawless letter has been retyped before it's presented for signature.

9. Is Your Company Free from Interdepartmental and Turf Wars?   If so, you have avoided a monumental barrier to competitive performance. If not, the cause of such barriers is likely to be a disconnected business process. Theoretically, all the elements of a company are supposed to cooperate toward achieving a common, understood goal. But in practice, each department becomes absorbed in making its own tasks easier, often disregarding the consequences of such changes on operations elsewhere in the company. The more the process disconnects, the more territorial managers inevitably become. What looks like a good idea where you work might cause problems down the line. Do you regularly consider that possibility?

10. Is Employee Turnover Low? You probably don't have access to personnel figures, but the grapevine estimate should be accurate enough for you to give a yes or no answer. In addition to the loss of productivity, high turnover inflicts excessive recruiting and training expense upon a company, and the sight of revolving-door employees takes a psychological toll among those who stay. For obvious reasons, turnover rate is a valid measure of corporate competitiveness.

11. Is Employee Morale High? This question ties in with the preceding one. Morale is directly proportional to competitiveness and to knowing where you stand as an individual employee. Because competitive companies use clear, relevant measurements of performance, individuals understand their assignments and, through feedback, possess a sense of accomplishment.

In competitive companies, employees usually exhibit enthusiasm for the mission at hand. A ready example of this phenomenon is, once again, Federal Express. If ever there was one, Fed Ex is a company where seconds count; yet you will rarely meet a Fed Ex employee who is too overwhelmed or too rushed to give detailed answers to any question a customer might ask.

12. Is Your Management Receptive to Change? You probably receive feedback on this issue all the time. When you make a suggestion, is it at least considered? Does management implement necessary changes in timely fashion, or do you, when looking up, behold the proverbial concrete ceiling?

13. Generally Speaking, Are You Free from Excessive Actions in Process, Too Many Meetings, and Multiple Sign-off Requirements? Most noncompetitive corporate procedures bury employees under a variety of nonvalue-added actions.

And, as I've already stated, job-related meetings and sign-offs, being time-consuming and bespeaking a belt-and-suspenders timidity, are also super indicators of an uncompetitive mindset. Who is afraid of what?

Do such procedures have a life of their own where you work? Whatever the case, the number of meetings and sign-offs tend to be inversely proportional to a company's competitiveness.

14. Generally Speaking, Do You Spend Your Time in Activity That Adds Value to the Company? No busywork? No distractions? A few? A lot? If your time is devoted to productive work, your company is effectively streamlined and, odds are, competitive.

Now, if you answered yes to *10 or more* of the above 14 questions, your company appears to be on the right track. If your yesses were *between 6 and 10*, there is vast room for improvement. If your score is *5 or below*, your company is in real trouble and hasn't a moment to lose.

A Competitive Atmosphere: Collective Bargaining versus Collective Interests

Few people could make their way through the above questions without chalking up some negative responses, because inevitably there are differences between what you expect from work and what your organization expects from you. It is just such differences that arouse classic management-versus-labor disputes. It's heartbreaking to witness such spectacles, in which factions whose overriding common interest in winning the time war lose sight of that objective and start sniping at each other. Organized labor and management can avoid such a trap by negotiating on the basis of what's fair rather than who's to blame. That tactic can work for you, too.

Reality Check _____

Subject: General Motors
Subject Industry: Automotive
Situation: As big and formidable as GM is, it has been clobbered by its inability to compete effectively. In other words, it has felt the sting of the time war. The issue at hand was whether one of GM's divisions should use inside or outside sources to supply needed components, and labor's representatives were opposed to the latter choice on the grounds that it would endanger GM workers' jobs. That being the case, the fundamental question was: What would make GM more competitive? The task here was able to demonstrate that all vested interests in this particular division were on the same side of that issue.

Outcome: As soon as both sides of the table accepted competitiveness as their common goal, the adversarial climate improved and matters of fairness took its place, whereupon the matter was resolved. In today's world, everyone at GM, white- and blue-collar, should be dedicated time warriors, united in the pursuit of competitiveness.

Another recent encounter, involving a Dallas service company, provides additional guidance on how big problems can be expeditiously handled. An employee who had been fired brought suit against the company, alleging that the termination was unfair. The dispute dragged on for months and consumed large amounts of time and money. When it came to trial, the beleaguered judge, knee-deep in unresolved disputes, declined to hear yet another case. Instead, he assigned the disputants to a mediator.

Professional conflict resolution is both an art and a science, but it is based upon the fact that disputants have one overriding common interest: reaching rapid and fair accord. At the first meeting, the assigned mediator made the astounding claim that 95 percent of his cases were resolved within 8 hours! He had each side state its case in 10 minutes, put each in a separate room, and thereafter went from room to room, asking questions. He then told each side the strengths and weaknesses of its case and proposed a solution he thought was fair. Both sides accepted. This troublesome matter thus vanished in less than a day because the mediator had ignored the contentious distractions of the case and brought his objectivity to bear on what both sides had in common: a fair solution. This is an exemplary case of short-cycle-time barrier removal.

What does all this have to do with you and the time war? Three things:

1. Concentrating on issues that merge your interest with that of your company's is a far more constructive way to achieve job satisfaction than itemizing grievances and using them as weapons. It is a method that will serve you well personally when you approach your boss about a performance agreement, or more frequent Cycles of Learning, or whatever other barriers lie between you and heightened job satisfaction. Always keep in mind—and point out—that it is in everyone's best interest to improve corporate competitiveness. The trick is to demonstrate that the improvements you seek are compatible with that objective. More about that later.

2. On a more general basis: if your company suffers from a contentious relationship between management and labor, conflict resolution techniques may be a constructive solution. The time saved in "problem solving" can be better spent on positive issues. It's all part of getting competitive.

3. Finally, it should be emphasized that classic management-versus-labor deadlocks rarely occur in short-cycle-time companies, where Cycles of Learning and regular feedback are part of the culture, because problems there surface faster and are dealt with before they become critical. When the processes are in good shape, so are the people. When the processes are in good shape, all the people—management and rank and file—realize that the enemy is not each other but the barriers that thwart better performance.

You Own Your Personal Competitiveness

A while back, I did a thumbnail computation of the value of my time as a company CEO. Based on the conservative assumption that my efforts added $2 million yearly to the bottom line, I was astounded to realize that that translated into 36 cents a second! Since then, whenever I'm stuck in a sluggish meeting, I'm haunted by those expensive seconds ticking by. If I'm unable to effect a change, I actually get unstuck from the situation as fast as I can and turn to something more profitable.

An owner should not get morbidly preoccupied with bottom lines lest he or she lose perspective on the value of life's other features, fishing, for example. But everyone, owner and otherwise, needs a precise notion of how much his or her time matters while on the job.

You can do the same kind of thumbnail estimate of what your time is worth. Most people, owners and otherwise, don't think about time that way, which is why there are so many "empty suits" in U.S. business. But to an extent, everyone is an owner. Think of your competitiveness as a form of property. If you refine it, that property appreciates. Ownership will always serve you well no matter where you go. It is, therefore, in your self-interest to improve those skills, and you should do all you can to see that your employer provides the ways and means for you to do so.

You may not be a leading stockholder in your company, but you are very definitely a shareholder in your own competitiveness.

Now think of that property—your competitiveness—as your personal weapon in the time war. Kept sharp and used with skill, your competitiveness can make an important difference in the fitness of your company. It is, therefore, in your employer's interest to hone your skills and remove obstructions to your best possible performance. You're in this together.

You are the owner of your personal competitiveness, which is your professional edge toward job security. Work to make the business process in your company give you the wherewithal to improve your competitive know-how. Everyone will benefit. You have a lot to gain.

How much is your personal competitiveness worth to your employer? Don't guess. Unless you're one of those "empty suits," the value you add is inherently greater than the monetary compensation you receive.

Computing Overall People Effectiveness

The more competitive your company is, the more effectively it uses its people. People effectiveness is measurable and is often used as a gauge of a company's fitness. You can compute your company's overall people effectiveness by dividing its shareholder value added (that is, its sales less material purchased, including resold outside services) plus profit by its total payroll cost (including fringe benefits). Resold outside services are whatever purchases your company makes that it passes along to a client with a slight markup. Consultant travel expenses are an example. The final figure should probably be between 2 and 5. The higher the number, the better the company is using its people resources to enhance shareholder value.

Computing Your Own Value Added

The above figure is of course a company average. On individual terms, *your* value added should be at least twice your salary plus fringe benefits if your company is competing effectively. In a really well-run company, your value added is probably three times that figure. Again, the higher the multiple, the more competitive you and your company are.

Now compute your value added down to the second. Let's assume that your company is well managed. If you're earning $30,000 a year and work a typical 2000 hours annually, your value-added figure could well be three times that: $90,000, or 1.25 cents a second. The next time you have a yen to linger over a coffee break or go outside to smoke a cigarette, consider that that second cup or that smoke is costing someone $7.50.

More important, keep your estimated value-added figure in mind the next time your assigned task seems to be bogging down. ("Ah, here's a barrier that's holding us up. The clock is ticking; what can I do?") Knowing how much he or she is contributing to the company should help anyone develop a new kind of respect for that ticking clock. Add more value and you add more self-respect.

Such thinking is all part of the new time warrior mindset, which includes looking at your job as part of a larger business process, not an entity unto itself. The average partner in my firm generates $5 a minute for the client. It is therefore unacceptable for that person to spend a few hours in an effort just to save us a few dollars, and everyone is expected to think that way. In the time war, you don't need a howitzer to kill a snake.

As easy as this point is to grasp, not many companies expect their employees to think in such terms. Only a small fraction of U.S. working people possess that mindset. I recently overheard a star salesman say he'd landed a $2 million sale, although he'd had to cut the price 10 percent to do so. The 10 percent he forfeited—$200,000—may have represented the entire profit on the transaction. With friends like that, his company doesn't need enemies! Perhaps this salesman should have thought in terms of material items instead of abstract percentages when he made that concession and asked himself, "Am I willing to give this customer eight Cadillacs to get the order?" That would have stopped me. Getting back to you: With so few people thinking competitively, acquiring the right mindset affords you an excellent opportunity to enhance your career.

Room for Improvement?

You have probably noticed that from the start, there has been the assumption that there's a great deal of untapped performance potential in your company which, if used, could win the war against time. It is equally true that there is a fail-safe method of improving performance to that level. I assume further that you are eager to enhance the time of your life through a better job environment and are willing to use your competitiveness as a weapon to achieve that goal.

It is not presumed that you have extraordinary talents or reserves of strength. The truth is, getting competitive is a matter of removing the barriers from your company's business and cultural processes, not extracting superhuman sacrifice and dedication from the work force.

People Are Not the Problem; Processes Are

Reality Check _____

Subject: U.S. Navy
Source: Tom Oliveri, TGI partner
Situation: This incident took place during 1970, when as a naval officer serving aboard a U.S. destroyer, Oliveri conducted a gunnery exercise against an onshore target.

OLIVERI: We were given both a set of target coordinates and a spotter to provide us feedback as to where our shell hit in relation to the target. I was stationed in the Combat Information Center (CIC) along with several enlisted personnel in order to manage communication from the spotter to our gunnery crews. We fired our first shell and waited anxiously to hear from the spotter. All we got was silence. I got on the radio and called up the spotter who responded with a "Hi there! Ready whenever you are!" Those of us in CIC exchanged questioning glances and decided that we might as well fire another shell at the original coordinates. After firing the second shell, we waited expectantly to hear from our spotter. Finally, the speaker in CIC crackled on, and a voice said simply, "You missed!"

I concluded quickly that this was not a particularly helpful piece of feedback. (One member of the crew asked if we had the coordinates for the *spotter*....Another crew member made several comments about the spotter's ancestry and mental capacity.)

I decided that it was time for another conversation with the spotter. I got the spotter on the radio again and asked if he had ever done this before. The response was "no." I then asked if anyone had explained to him what was expected of a spotter. This time the response was a somewhat forlorn "Not really." At this point I proceeded to explain what this exercise was about and to educate him as to the type of feedback we were expecting. We proceeded to fire a third shell at the original coordinates. This time, the voice on the speaker responded with a loud and clear, "On line, one zero zero yards short." After providing this information to the gunnery crew, we fired our fourth shell. The feedback was "On line, two zero yards short." We hit the target with the fifth shell.

Conclusion

OLIVERI: Although I never met the spotter, I'm sure that he was far more pleased with the outcome than if we had tried to put a shell in his lap. I am also confident that at his next opportunity, he got it right the first time....It is probably clear that if we had put our feedback system in place properly to begin with, we could have hit the target with the third shell instead of the fifth.

The important lesson from this story has to do with how we react when we get what appears to be a really stupid piece of feedback.

There is a natural human tendency to assume that anyone who provides useless and/or idiotic feedback must be useless, or an idiot, or a useless idiot, so we write the person off as a potential source of information, as was almost done with the spotter in Tom's story.

But experience proves that if you fix the process, the people will do just fine. If you get feedback that is useless or unresponsive to your needs, find out why and fix the process, don't write off the sender.

Reality Check

Subject: A Philips Semiconductor plant in the Netherlands
Source: John Schramm, TGI partner
Situation

SCHRAMM: The manufacturing manager was skeptical and not too receptive of TCT methods. Some folks viewed him as an obstacle to progress when in fact he was a very capable, hard-working manager...but not too cooperative.

(John decided that the problem here was the poor processes of the plant, not the manager. Accordingly, he decided to let the merits of short cycle time correct the processes and let personality matters take care of themselves.)

SCHRAMM: For several weeks, I cultivated the manager via suggestions as related to his objectives—*not legislation*. In fact, I gave him weekly lists of suggestions to improve current performance and what the result might be. I told him to pick a few each week and try them. This he did, and progress toward goals began. He became a good friend, competent fabrication manager, and ultimately was promoted to his boss's job.

Outcome: The results were instructive all around.

SCHRAMM: The client met its cycle time and yield goals. The consulting team learned that people who appear to be

barriers are not always so. In fact, in many cases, the
most competent client personnel are the most problem
initially—they feel threatened. Once that person's hot button
is found—and the consulting team can set an example—he
or she becomes a tremendous asset and the project
progresses.

People are not the problem. Processes are.

4

Avoiding Time Traps

Crisis and Opportunity

These days, everyone from the White House down talks about the United States' "crisis of competitiveness." The reason for the fretful publicity is the well-founded fear that U.S. companies are fumbling the ball in world markets. We seem to have lost the ability to seize opportunities, to make products that are reliable and attractive, and to offer our wares at acceptably low prices. The nation's trade deficit has mushroomed alarmingly. It is uncertain whether beleaguered U.S. companies can recapture the competitive edge they once enjoyed. In industries that produce cars, steel, and semiconductors, the United States' one-time clear pre-eminence may be gone forever. Meanwhile, the pace of business is accelerating, increasing the time pressures on every company. Future uncertainties make competitiveness an issue of crisis proportions.

The current competitiveness crisis is loaded with opportunity. Every company in the nation has the potential to improve its performance substantially — without adding new resources.

Such potential has always existed, because U.S. industry has *never* operated up to its capabilities. The truth is that in the so-called good old days, the nation's vaunted productivity was relative: Americans outperformed foreign competitors whose methods were woefully unproductive. The U.S. industrial miracle of World War II was indeed impressive, but it was the wartime ravaging of other nations' industrial bases, not some unique Yankee know-how, that won U.S. industry its postwar dominance. Those advantages couldn't last forever. The rules have changed worldwide. As the pace of business and technological change quickens, the life expectancy of every product and service shortens. The need is now, which is why timely customer service is a keystone of true competitiveness. Companies that cannot quicken their response to changing demand will decline. It's that simple.

The future belongs to organizations, U.S. or otherwise, that shorten their processes, adopt the mindset of barrier removal, and use their resources to maximum advantage through Cycles of Learning. The improvement potential represented by the proper use of these resources is enormous. If you and your company exploit that opportunity, you can win the historic war against time.

Obviously, winning the time war by making your company competitive takes more than willpower and upbeat morale. Winning requires a precise and predictable system: Total Cycle Time is one. Implementing that system is not easy, but its principles are a cinch to grasp.

A National Tendency to Lose the Competitive Edge

Assessing corporate performance levels and providing prescriptions for improvement is my business. My product is results that produce competitiveness. Most of these are brought about by barrier removal: streamlining business processes and organizational culture so that resources are used more effectively. I have never encountered a single company in which people were performing at their potential. Not on production lines, not in design groups, not in services, nor in marketing — nowhere. The condition is critical, but luckily, there is a remedy.

Nearly all businesses admit they have room for improvement. They have even more room than they realize, because almost all are overestimating their actual performance, measuring the wrong things, and perpetuating procedures that obstruct improvement. Over the years, as their business systems evolve, companies typically retain procedures that time has rendered obsolete. And as companies grow, they add new procedures and resources without weeding out old, now-redundant ones. The same applies to ideas: last year's conceptual breakthroughs may lose their relevance, but having meanwhile acquired a life of their own, they are retained. To add to the confusion, changing leadership produces an overlay of various management systems and styles. In other words, the natural process of corporate growth results in a maze of entrenched procedures, hidebound attitudes, non-value-added steps, far too many actions in process, and long feedback loops, all of which make effective performance impossible.

Five Basic Conditions Producing Barriers

Those procedures, attitudes, steps, and practices are the enemy of competition. To win the time war, they must be rooted out and destroyed, or they will severely damage any company that tolerates their continued presence. Finding and blasting away these barriers is your duty as a time warrior. As soon as you know more about the origins and types of various barriers, you should get started. As you will see, freeing yourself and your organization of such barriers can make a colossal difference in your professional well-being.

Barriers owe their existence to five basic conditions, each one of which is reviewed below. They are:

- Long cycle times
- Faulty measurements
- Improper quality improvement programs

- Cultural myopia
- Management by crisis

The Cycle Time Trap

One of the most important indicators of performance is *cycle time* — the time it takes to perform a task from beginning to end. As the number of required procedures and steps increases within a company or a job, driving up the actions in process, cycle times lengthen, and the ability to provide customers with timely service declines accordingly. It takes longer to process an order, or to get a purchase authorized, or to design a component, or to build it. It gets harder to make accurate forecasts, because with lengthening cycle times, planners have to look farther and farther into the future. To make matters worse, Cycles of Learning become fewer and farther between and so do their benefits.

Companies with long cycle times should not blame their shortcomings on outside factors. Until these companies eliminate the internal barriers to competitive performance, they and their people are living on borrowed time.

It goes without saying that every time warrior must be ruthless in spotting and battling practices, procedures, and attitudes that needlessly lengthen cycle times. Except in the most competitive companies, true time warriors are quite rare. Likewise, most managers believe that their accustomed performance is the best they can achieve without adding resources. The mentality of "If it ain't broke, don't fix it" prevails. They should have another look. It *is* broken.

The Faulty Measurements Trap

It is easy for managers to kid themselves. Few companies use measurements that reveal their true level of performance. Some, for example, compare themselves to competitors without asking whether such rivals are performing up to potential. In fact, there are entire industries in which performance runs from poor to awful and in which the merely poor performers are considered stars! Other companies may measure the right things the wrong way—by fudging, miscalculating, or misinterpreting their results. Often, employees are measured by the problems they solve rather than the problems they *prevent*. The negative effects of such practices compounds over time.

The Quality Trap

The pursuit of higher quality is, ironically, often to blame for uncompetitive performance. Product improvement is a laudable goal, and in these times of heightening competition, a necessary one. But unfortunately, quality improvement is usually identified as an end in itself, out of context with other corporate measurements.

The truth is that good quality is the natural result of business processes that are barrier-free and competitive.

Every quality program should be driven by an effort to cut cycle times, not a long list of independent "excellence criteria."

One reason the quality trap is widespread is an overabundance of independent "quality experts" with academic rather than business backgrounds: people inexperienced in practical management who therefore do not grasp the relationship of quality to the functional business process. The same is true for the new crop of MBA-equipped greenhorns.

Ill-advised and apparently lulled by the feel-good aspects of quality improvement, many troubled organizations draw up a quality dream list on which they pin their hopes for competitiveness. They are barking up the wrong tree. Their quality problems result from faulty business processes in the functional area.

Allocating precious resources to meet arbitrarily imposed improvement standards will complicate business processes further. And because quality is a function of the business process, it may well decline, not improve, in the long run.

The Cultural Myopia Trap

The biggest and subtlest barriers are cultural, part of a company's shared values, traditions, myths, style, and self-image. Corporate culture influences strategic decisions, product selection, public relations, and employee morale.

Some of the best companies pride themselves on their distinctive cultures, and there can be quite a variety within the same industry. For example, in the world of electronics, Texas Instruments is legendary for its highly disciplined, technology-driven, almost totalitarian environment. At TI, planning and strategy require a huge chunk of management time, and the trick is to give breathing space to spontaneity.

There is more diversity at Motorola, TI's leading rival, because discipline in that corporation is far weaker: Managers are used to challenging orders from above or interpreting them freely. Those diametrically opposed environments each possess certain advantages, and both TI and Motorola attribute much of their success to their cultural uniqueness.

The stronger the culture, however, the more a company looks inward, which invites self-deception, resistance to outside influence, and the accumulation of counterproductive practices. Cultural assumptions blur vision to a point where it becomes hard to see the trees for the forest. But rest assured: The forest is full of barriers that lengthen cycle time, retard performance, complicate work, and make employees' lives miserable. Dismantle those barriers, and working life—*your* working life—will improve dramatically.

The Management-by-Crisis Trap

Even allowing for cultural myopia, why aren't more road-blocks detected and destroyed as a matter of course? Isn't it management's job to make a company run as smoothly as possible? Theoretically, it is. But many managers, most, perhaps, operate in a perpetual crisis mode that saps their creativity. Here is a typical sequence:

1. Crisis Creates Urgency. Too many business executives enter their offices each morning only to be ambushed by a swarm of crises demanding their attention. These are usually questions regarding deliverables:

- Can a tardy shipment be speeded up?

- Can a revised quotation on potential business be submitted at the last minute?

- Can a winning paragraph be inserted into a sales letter?

- Can some special effort be made to accelerate a preferred customer's order?

Confronting such pop-up crises is exhausting and distracting — unless the managers involved *created* them in the first place.

2. Urgency Creates Anxiety. Such crises also create a high-pressure, nerve-wracking environment in which managers devote the lion's share of their time to the most bothersome issues, such as cantankerous customers, insubordinate employees, government regulators, or agile competitors who are outmaneuvering them in the marketplace. Constantly in firefighting mode, they can't address themselves to whatever is causing the fires.

3. Anxiety Sucks Up Resources. Meanwhile, in a heroic attempt to deliver the expected goods or services, such managers call for reinforcements: more equipment, more time, more people, more inventory, more consultants, more emergency programs. Regrettably, this course of action is self-defeating. In the long run, it complicates business, increases administrative chores, and lengthens cycle times. And it is expensive! There may be more firefighting equipment on line, but fires continue to flare up. So do ulcers.

4. Stress Blocks Vision.   Under stress, a manager has more and more difficulty identifying and removing the entrenched sources of these problems: the barriers to straightforward performance. Take the following case: It is urgent for a manager to provide precise delivery of orders to a preferred customer. To ensure this, he increases the allotted production time to allow for possible slipups, only to find that his extended delivery date is unacceptable. Whereupon, to ensure on-time delivery in the future, he batch-processes surplus quantities of bread-and-butter items only to have the customer change the next order's specifications. In both instances, this manager's immediate need to satisfy customers, beat out the competition, and extract whatever it takes from his employees gives him no time to consider how he might escape the perpetual round of short-term crises.

5. Process and Cultural Barriers Impede Progress. Managers continue to patch and repatch their areas of responsibility while the cause of most of their problems—high inventory levels, unbalanced production lines, improper scheduling techniques, time-consuming inspections, interruptions, and overzealous controls, to name a few—go unattended.

Reality Check: Substitute Process _____

Subject Industry: Chemicals
Situation: A good example of an unattended substitute process barrier turned up inside a producer of chemically based products that had to meet rigorous government testing. In the case of one important product, first-pass yield was very

poor. Nonetheless, the company managed to keep its volume high thanks to a chemist who could tweak the product up to standard using his esoteric know-how. This individual's ability to counteract low yield had made him a corporate hero, and he was rewarded for his efforts.

An assessment of the situation lead to the chemist's "heroism" being challenged. In lieu of changing the company's faulty business process for the better, he was using his subject matter expertise to work around it. Rewarding such deeds virtually guaranteed that the substitute process would stay in place.

Conclusion: Once top management was convinced to reward the removal of process barriers rather than the ability to circumvent them, the chemist turned his talents to finding a lasting solution.

The hierarchical impact of barriers can be awesome. A single cultural barrier (such as a territorial tradition in which managers "protect" their own turf) can prevent 10 sets of general procedural improvements, which may in turn prevent a hundred improvements at individuals' subject matter level.

Getting out of this rut requires managers and their subordinates to rise above the nagging problems that are eating them alive and consider their company's entire business process. Only then will the underlying barriers that cause their daily frustration be exposed. How is this to be done? By systematic use of Cycles of Learning. By improving first-pass yield. By eliminating the non-value-added rigmarole of daily effort.

Cutting the Gordian Knot

Ironically, the largest barriers—those that impact the business process or the fundamental culture of your company—are often the most subtle. They come in all shapes and sizes: faulty command structure, unnecessary repetition, excessive paperwork, improper use of machinery, and overzealous inspections, among them. They are so much a part of everyday activity that only a small percentage can be readily identified.

So long as they go unchallenged, however, competitiveness is impossible. Ridding your company of such barriers usually requires the pooled experience of seasoned workers across the company, people who despite their different everyday functions share the same frustrations and can see both the forest and the trees. Even then, however, cross-functional teams may not get far, because only a few big barriers (about 30 percent) can be removed without placing the status quo under severe stress. There is thus an understandable tendency among problem-solving teams to avoid overstraining an embattled system.

The noble but frustrating efforts of a troubled corporation to cure its own ills are like those of an ailing doctor who tries self-medication but fails to get better. In both cases, objectivity is the missing ingredient. If it is determined to go the distance, an ailing company must almost always call in outside change specialists who are not wedded to established practices or blinded by corporate mythology. Although it is seldom pleasant for insiders to admit how embedded their barriers are, the fact remains that outsiders can accelerate barrier removal while helping their clients acquire a more productive cultural mindset.

Reality Check _____

Subject Process: Order Entry
Subject Industry: Manufacturing
Source: Lou Howitz, TGI partner
Situation: Howitz made a verbal report, supported by hand-generated exhibits, to the manager of materials. He was very pleased. The report was subsequently used by the manager of the Order Processing Department to *self-medicate*.
Outcome: Unfortunately, the order entry manager did not understand how to calculate cycle time properly. As a result, instead of prompting a decline, his mistakes added another seven days to his department's cycle time within a month.

That sort of thing happens all too often when companies forgo the outsider option. But bear in mind the need for *seasoned* outsiders. Other types can do more harm than good. As is the case with the quality trap, there are too many "competitiveness experts" who peddle single, incomplete solutions or novel managerial concepts: "quality control," "people involvement," "matrix management," or what have you. Piecemeal approaches do not get at the fundamentals of competitiveness, nor do they change your mindset or your company's. Make no mistake, retaining the competitive edge is a matter of adopting a *total* approach, which includes the permanent acceptance of short-cycle-time thinking as the cornerstone of corporate culture.

Halfway measures that zero in on quality, or customer service, or productivity, or various management problems, treat the object of their focus as though it were a single issue independent of other factors. The best that approach can do is create a *temporary appearance* of good performance: quality may rise, productivity may improve, and deliveries may be according to schedule — for a while.

Are you able to see a difference between the appearance and the reality of high performance? Has your company's attempt to keep pace with the competition made your job more challenging and interesting? If something seems to be missing, you are working below your entitlement. You're not getting your fair share of the job excitement.

A New Mindset: Total Cycle Time

Being excited about work is part of the alternative mindset. Total Cycle Time is a cultural change, not a quick cure. What is the mindset where you work? In discussing your company's performance potential, have you heard any of the following statements?

- "We need to add more people!"
- "We need enough inventory to fill any order!"
- "We need to slow down and build a better product!"

Wrong! That's the apply-resources mentality. It is as prevalent in government agencies, universities, nonprofit foundations, and the service sector as it is in manufacturing-based business. And unfortunately, because it's pervasive, you probably *haven't* heard:

- "Our productivity is better, and with less investment!"
- "Our customer service is better, and with less inventory!"
- "Our quality is better because our products take less time to make!"

Right! See the difference? The first set reveals a cultural impulse to throw resources at problems, the results of which create the *appearance* of effective performance. The second bespeaks a determination to restructure the process to achieve real-world competitiveness.

The future belongs to companies who see the need for short cycle times. These companies are determined to reduce the time it takes to complete every discrete activity within their organization: develop a product, manufacture a product, deliver a service, type a letter, enter an order, procure materials, acquire a subsidiary, install a factory, reduce costs, change a culture—everything.

Total Cycle Time is the combined effect of the cycle times of all business processes in an organization, from the time a customer need is expressed until it is satisfied.

The word *total* is also a reminder that to be competitive, every working part of every business must reduce cycle time, reduce actions in process, apply Cycles of Learning, remove barriers, learn to do the assigned task right the first time, install the right measurements, and make a permanent cultural commitment to keeping things that way.

Bottom Lines: Total Cycle Time's Impact

The method of Total Cycle Time is to identify, measure, and analyze each individual cycle of activity within a company so that work can be simplified. Within the manufacturing cycle, best characterized as the make/market loop, there are numerous "subloops" between entering an order and the collecting for the final product. Most companies also have a design/development loop which likewise embraces many subloops. With Total Cycle Time, every loop and subloop is studied, using performance records, diagnostic techniques, and accumulated know-how. Actions in process are cut. Barriers and substitute processes are identified and removed. Cycle times fall, making the company responsive to customers. Meanwhile, the new ethic is internalized so that short-cycle-time thinking permeates the organization and becomes an integral part of the culture.

If you follow the *steps* outlined in this chapter, you will be able to analyze your own task, whether it be a sub- or sub-subloop, and start to eliminate the obstructions to better, more rewarding personal performance.

Total Cycle Time and the Performance Continuum

The barriers that lurk at every level in a company and the mindset that lets them stay in place are the reasons your company may not be operating up to its potential. Because of the failure to recognize barriers all around, there is also a failure to recognize the gap between your accustomed performance and your true potential.

Baseline

The habitual, routine level of a company's performance, called *baseline*, is seldom an accurate reflection of true capability. The reason for this disparity is the incremental approach to improvement which typifies U.S. business. Thinking incrementally, most managers and workers who are getting by may concede that there is room for some slight enhancement of their performance: "I can do 5 percent better than last year," or "I might be able to chop a day off my 30-day cycle time." And, of course, if some recent setback has dropped performance below baseline, people will concede that recovery is possible — back to baseline, of course. Very few, however, ask themselves, "What is the absolute *best* I might achieve, and how do I get to it?"

Baseline performance goes unchallenged because employees and executives are used to working at that level. It is never a true indicator of a company's performance potential.

Benchmark

If your company thinks incrementally, its improvement objectives are of a type I call *benchmark*. Such goals may be based on the superior performance of a competitor, in which case it becomes your task to catch that rival. If your benchmark is set a notch higher, and you reach it, your company can claim to be number 1. But since all of your competitors are probably nowhere near *their* true performance potential, being number 1 is like being the tallest kid, still not a true adult. Why set your goal at someone else's baseline? Think of the outcome had Federal Express used the U.S. Postal Service as its benchmark!

Benchmarking is apt to be quite inaccurate because its reference points are inaccurate. At baseline, most companies appear to be performing better than they are because they often manipulate their own measurements. Thus, neither your company's figures nor those of its rivals should be taken as a precise guide to potential performance.

To underline the point, a corporation I once encountered was able to tweak its definition of on-time delivery enough to claim a 90 percent effectiveness rate. The real percentage was more like 40, as its frustrated customers could confirm. In another case, managers had massaged their data to a point where they claimed a first-pass yield of 92 percent. Objective measurements showed 30!

Benchmark is a long way from what is possible. Don't confuse the industry's "best" with your actual potential.

Entitlement

Your real-time actual potential is your *entitlement*: the best performance you can routinely achieve using the resources at your disposal. Why settle for improvement goals of 5 percent if you can improve by 10 times that factor? When you and your organization start to think in those terms, you will have escaped the incremental hangup, which is a real breakthrough. Instead of asking yourself if a 5 or 6 percent performance improvement is attainable, consider what you might do in the best circumstances with your available resources. When looking at a 30-day baseline cycle time, instead of plotting how to reduce it by a day or two, consider how you might knock it down to a day or two. Such improvements leave the benchmark mentality in the dust. They can be accurately estimated, and they *are* achievable.

Entitlement is the best performance you can get with today's resources or less.

Entitlement is continuously improvable through feedback from Cycles of Learning.

Between baseline and entitlement, where entrenched barriers still exist, throwing new money and people into an operation is counterproductive. Save your money. Just say no!

Enhanced Entitlement (Your Strategic Best)

Improved performance, of course, can continue beyond the original entitlement goal. By selectively adding resources after reaching entitlement, a company (or an individual) can raise its entitlement level and rate of continuous improvement. The trick, however, is to know how and where to add the resources. Such wisdom is acquired during the process of reaching entitlement.

Enhanced entitlement is achievable only after reaching entitlement with the resources on hand.

It is the highest step in the performance continuum. Having maximized the effectiveness of existing resources, your company can now make wise decisions about where to apply new resources.

The Impact of Total Cycle Time

Total Cycle Time is how you get from baseline to entitlement. Here are some statistical results showing the kind of impact Total Cycle Time can produce:

- It can reduce the time needed to bring a new product or service to market by at least 30 and sometimes by as much as 70 percent.

- It can increase return on assets between 20 and 100 percent.

- It can increase rank-and-file productivity 10 to 30 percent; but in the white-collar sector (which has traditionally been neglected as a problem area), the improvement potentials range as high as 100 percent or more.

These numbers become even more remarkable in light of the following facts:

- These improvements in performance are attainable with the resources on hand. In fact, they are often attainable with fewer than your current resources. They require *no* new expenditures.

- These improvements in performance create an environment in which you become more productive while working at your accustomed pace. They require *no* speeding up on the part of the work force.

Small wonder senior managers greet such news with smiles and shrugs. Nor can any self-respecting person, blue- or white-collar, be expected to jump at the notion that there is so much slack in current performance. It sounds a bit insulting, and some are bound to take it personally. Nevertheless, it's true.

So, the baseline-entitlement gap contains some bad news and some good news:

- The bad news: Your company presently tolerates all manner of non-value-added steps—barriers—that are dramatically retarding its performance potential.

- The good news: Becoming dynamic and outmaneuvering the competition—with the appropriate financial results—is within your company's grasp without any outlay for new resources.

The impact of Total Cycle Time, then, is substantial in most companies and colossal in quite a few. In some cases, it has literally made the difference between corporate life and death.

Reality Check _____

Subject Company: NBK Corporation
Source: Jim Newton, president of NBK, hired to turn things around
Situation: In 1983, NBK Corporation had serious cash problems and was near bankruptcy. A cycle time reduction program was initiated for the purpose of generating some of the required cash and improving NBK's service.

NEWTON: For the next year and a half, NBK underwent a program to reduce its manufacturing and marketing cycle time. By the end of 1984, cycle time had been reduced from about 85 days to about 20 days—including order processing. In addition, the accounts receivable collections cycle was improved by about 20 days.

Cash flow improved accordingly, providing NBK with 60 percent of the survival funds it needed. That was the open sesame; the rest came from venture investors and conversions to debt or payables by major vendors of raw materials to NBK. The cash flow from the cycle time program provided the credibility to obtain needed concessions from the vendors and the bank.

By the end of 1984, NBK was healthy enough to attract interested buyers who might safely grow the company. By mid-1985, it had been acquired for about $12.5 million. Thus, the cycle time reduction can be given the majority of the credit for converting a worthless asset (a company going under) into a $12.5 million asset which was sold. It was the major factor in maintaining 100-plus jobs for the period by allowing the company to survive.

At the time of the sale, the president and his key staff members were asked to sign 3-year employment contracts—another bonus of the successful program. Cycle time reduction has the potential to generate a very large share of the cash needs even of a company in trouble. The improved cash flow multiplies the value of the company substantially.

For you, reaching entitlement promises a job where obstructions are removed, where you see the results of your own work, and where there is true job security in the assurance that your company will be around for a while.

Adopting the culture of Total Cycle Time is much like opting for a program of supervised weight loss instead of a two-week miracle diet. Although sticking to a proper diet may not be easy, you will shed pounds if you follow the guidelines set out by your doctor. But that is not the end of your responsibility. Keeping the lost weight off requires behavior modification. You must acquire *and permanently retain* a different discipline about eating. It's the same with Total Cycle Time: You must be vigilant to avoid relapsing into your old bad habits.

Additional Rewards of Entitlement

Until their companies go into the inevitable tailspin, base-liners and incremental thinkers are fat and happy. Entitlement people, by contrast, are slim and *very* happy. At entitlement, your self-esteem is enhanced, and rightly so, because you are part of a competitive team that is getting quick results and using resources to maximum advantage. Accordingly, you can expect to be recognized, possibly promoted, and your job options increased. Best of all, perhaps, you acquire the self-confidence and peace of mind that come from being ahead of the rat race.

Three Modeling Steps to Determine Your Entitlement

Recently, my firm was invited to Chicago to chart entitlement for a $500 million company that builds 12,000 railroad cars a year. There were, of course, no precedents for such a program. We were able to undertake the task confidently, however, thanks to modeling.

Modeling can assist the biggest and smallest assessments of entitlement—the smallest being on the individual level. You can use a simplified version of the corporate assessment to determine personal baseline and entitlement.

You begin by estimating your baseline cycle time. Unless you work at a very straightforward task, this can be tricky. In fact, it is the inability to compute actual cycle times accurately that permits managers to rationalize poor performance levels, believing they are doing better than they are. Follow the next four steps and you'll avoid that pitfall.

1. What Is Your Baseline?

Your first step is to define when your particular task begins and ends. Be systematic: List every step that is part of your job. Then prepare a simple flow diagram depicting how these various tasks interlock with the rest of your company's process.

The next step is to get a hard number on the actions in process you must perform within your own business process. You accomplish this by listing personal activities you perform. If yours is a white-collar job, these might include completing telephone calls, reading reports, preparing proposals, filing, or whatever. Add up the number of actions in process. When you have done so, divide that figure by the number of actions completed in a given period of time. That is your baseline cycle time.

Continuing with the white-collar example above, look at your desk. You may have 20 items waiting to be worked on. If you can complete 4 per day (your output rate) and you are receiving an average of 6 per day (your input rate), your paperwork cycle time is 4 days and going up (20 divided by 5).

2. What Is Your First-Pass Yield?

First-pass yield is probably the best measure of the quality of a business process. It is the percentage of actions involved in your specific task that you complete perfectly on the first attempt.

You will need to know what percentage of every step is completed perfectly on the first attempt. If, for instance, you have a sloppy process with many steps that don't follow a meaningful sequence, you may sometimes miss a step, inadvertently complete a step too soon or too late, or even repeat a step. That, of course, causes rework, which undermines first-pass yield. If you have to put things on hold now and then before completing them properly, your first-pass yield is lowered, and your processes are almost certainly faulty.

It's important not to overestimate your first-pass yield. Take telephone efficiency, for example: If for every 10 calls that you dial, you misdial one, get a wrong number and have to redial, or you hear that irritating disembodied voice telling you "your call cannot be completed as dialed," you are faced with rework, and your telephone first-pass yield drops to 90 percent. But suppose in addition that while placing one of those ten calls you realize at the last second that you have dialed incorrectly, so you hang up in the nick of time and do it right. Although you have avoided a wrong connection, you have nonetheless also lost time to rework. Your first-pass yield has now dropped to 81 percent because of the two basic failures.

Be sure you have not overlooked all the instances of rework. It is easy to overestimate first-pass yield and become complacent about performance.

3. What Is Your Entitlement?

You will next need to analyze your actions in process to see where they can be streamlined. Examine that stack of paper on your desk, or whatever requests for action that enter your work space every day. Does this work load arrive at a regular pace? Are you occasionally overwhelmed because someone up the line sends you work in batches? Whatever the case, you should reexamine the validity of actions in process. Ask yourself,

- Does completing this action add value to the company and its business?

- Does this action improve the company's response to customers?

- Does this action accelerate results?

- Does this action improve the effective use of resources on hand?

- If not, why am I doing it?

- Do I have the authority to get rid of this action?

Remember that you are the world's leading expert on your personal work slot. Accordingly, you are the one who will see the close-in barriers that make your work a grind. Moreover, you are probably empowered to change such things for the better. Think of that ticking clock, and see how you could simplify your process.

Although you are the expert in your own job's particular subject matter, you nonetheless have much room for improvement. Everyone at baseline does. I can assure you that, at entitlement, subject matter gains in individual productivity are about 15 percent in blue-collar jobs and at least 50 percent in white-collar.

To complete your entitlement estimate, you will need to examine the overall business process with which your flow chart connects. The chart will help you discern the steps that lie outside your immediate work space. Which ones have a negative effect on the completion of your work? Estimate the impact on your cycle time and first-pass yield if those barriers were eliminated. Again, the criteria are:

- Does this step add value?
- If not, whose responsibility is it to eliminate the barrier?
- If eliminating the barrier lies beyond my own area of responsibility, what can I do to challenge it?

You will now be bumping into those large barriers that bedevil your company's overall business operation. As you will see in Chapter 5, your greatest strides in slashing cycle time will come when those business process and cultural barriers are removed. Meanwhile, don't be surprised by the gap between your estimated baseline and entitlement; that's the name of the game.

Using Historical Performance and Theoretical Cycle Time to Determine Entitlement

It is quite possible that you have overlooked some barriers whose removal would make a big difference in your entitlement figure. With that in mind, you should utilize two other methods of computing entitlement: *historical performance* and *theoretical cycle time*. These added exercises will allow you to approximate entitlement realistically.

If you have records of past performance, they can be a great help in determining entitlement. Search out the extremes of your performance cycle times—the longest and shortest—and examine them for clues about what caused those variations. For example, what actions were included in the long cycles but not in the short?

Your entitlement cycle time is almost always close to your shortest performance time. Thus, if your best-case performance was, say, 45 minutes and your worst 5 hours, you can be reasonably certain that your entitlement—the performance level you can *routinely* expect to achieve—is around 45 minutes!

There is a third way to crosscheck your entitlement: theoretical cycle time.

Theoretical cycle time is the time it would take you to complete every stage of a single assigned action if there were no waiting, stopping, setup time, mistakes, rework, or delays of any kind.

Calculating theoretical cycle time requires care. You have already divided your assigned task into its component parts. Use your flowchart to clarify these. This time, isolate all the no-value steps and subtract the time they require from your baseline. That process eliminates the time you waste on each and every barrier. Your goal is to isolate the back-to-back process time necessary to complete value-added actions from beginning to end, no more.

The better you are at computing theoretical cycle time, the more it is likely to surprise you, especially if you work at a white-collar job where there is characteristically more non-value-added time than elsewhere. It is not at all unusual for a theoretical figure to be but 5 or 10 percent of baseline. Of course, the theoretical figure is just that. Your real-world entitlement will inevitably fall somewhere between your theoretical and your baseline figures. Although figures vary according to individual circumstances, experience reveals that entitlement is almost always between two and three times theoretical.

By comparing your estimates based upon the removal of existing barriers, your high-low historical performance, and your figure for theoretical, you can zero in on an entitlement figure. If you have calculated carefully, that range of improvement is a far cry from your baseline calculation (it always is). Now, if you multiply your improvement at entitlement by the number of cycles and subcycles within your company, you can certainly see that there is enormous room for improvement.

If you have not already done so, I recommend that you work through the above steps at this point. There will be more discussion about your personal entitlement in Chapters 7 and 8, and the work you have done will come in handy. Meanwhile, the exercise will have made you a believer.

Ready for Battle?

Now, imagine how much more effective you will be when you become a time warrior and remove the barriers to your personal entitlement. Imagine how much more rewarding your work will be once you are free to concentrate on what really matters. Imagine how much more effective your company would be if everyone in it were a time warrior.

The crisis of competitiveness is real. It is a scramble for time which only the quickest can win. But the time war is full of opportunity. The road to victory is the road from baseline to entitlement. Don't train your sights or waste your ammunition on targets outside your company; the enemies lie within. Regardless of the world situation — recession, inflation, Japan Inc., and the nation's trade policies — you and your company have plenty of room to improve and plenty of effective weapons to bring about that improvement.

5

Clearing the Way to Entitlement

However they came to be, performance barriers can be grouped into four categories:

1. Subject matter
2. Business process
3. Culture
4. Substitute process

Achieving entitlement means defeating all four types wherever they occur.

Overcoming Subject Matter Barriers

Subject matter barriers are associated with the particular aspects of your company's business or the skills you as an individual possess. They are thus not difficult for a seasoned, dedicated insider to spot. By the same token, these barriers are usually the easiest ones to eliminate because of your personal expertise. No matter what your task may be, unless you've just started you are an expert in its execution, which makes you an effective barrier remover in your immediate vicinity.

Back in the seventies, my specialty was solving various manufacturing problems within the semiconductor industry.

Knowing the ins and outs of that—or any—business is an example of subject matter expertise. Likewise, you owe your professional career to whatever skill you have developed in your own specialty. If you've completed the work prescribed in Chapter 4 and have flowcharted the order of your activity, you've probably already spotted a hang-up or two. If, for example, you're on a manufacturing line, you might have zeroed in on an unreliable piece of equipment whose downtime prevents work from proceeding evenly. Or if you're in an office, you might have decided that your word-processing software doesn't have the features you need to work efficiently. When you critically examine every step of your actions in process, you will probably uncover quite a few needless, non-value-added obstructions.

A group of managers I recently addressed were asked to raise their hands if their secretaries delivered mail to their desks two or more times a day. No hands. Asked how many got mail once a day, hands went up all around. They were all victims of a performance barrier. "Once-a-day delivery," I told them, "is certainly convenient for secretaries, but it automatically builds a half-day delay into every piece of mail. In other words, your effective cycle time increases by at least half a day! Why put up with this?" Quite a few barriers of that sort can go undetected if you don't examine every step of your activity. Perhaps the following examples will jump-start your progress:

- Do you put off certain tasks until Monday so that you can "get a fresh start" on them at the beginning of each week? (If so, you could be lengthening your average cycle time by half a week.)

- Might it make more sense for you to drop off a piece of completed paperwork on your way to lunch instead of putting it in the interoffice mail?

- If you use the telephone a lot, do you find yourself engaged in ceremonial chitchat or socializing? (It is possible to be courteous without tying up time in non-value-added conversation, and the person on the other end of the line knows that too.)

Scheduled business meetings offer a golden opportunity to cut cycle time. Your first step, of course, is to determine whether such meetings add value to your responsibility and avoid them if they don't. If you're in charge of a legitimate meeting that usually takes an hour, why not reduce the allotted time to forty minutes? Meetings have a way of expanding to fill the time reserved for them; rarely do they end early. It never ceases to amaze me how meetings can turn a roomful of intelligent people into something less than the sum of its parts, with negative results for all. This is war! Instead of padding the time, resolve in advance to get through your agenda sooner than is customary, and inform other participants in advance about your intent.

Reality Check _____

Subject: Wasteful Meetings
Source: Jan Barnard, TGI partner
Situation

BARNARD: A company general manager sent out an agenda to his staff that the subject of next week's meeting would be communication, and would they each come prepared to discuss the topic? At the meeting the following week, they each came prepared (indeed)!...The director of Engineering had a presentation on the system they had in development which was going to be introduced the following month. The director of Finance and Administration came prepared to discuss the new E-mail system the company had just purchased. The Sales and Marketing manager wanted to talk about the advertising program that had been put together for the new product announcement the following month, and the Human Resources manager brought copies of the just-published "State of the Company" VCR tape that was being sent to each employee. The Manufacturing manager thought it was about time they talked about the fact that Engineering wasn't talking to Manufacturing as they were transferring new products into Manufacturing. The general manager wanted to talk about forming a cross-functional team to bring new products to market.... This shows what happens when communications are not clear, as well as when each functional operation has its own set of priorities and goals.

Conclusion: Think of the time that meeting wasted because the agenda was not made clear beforehand. And when the confusion became obvious, where were the time warriors? You may not chair corporate-level summit conferences, but whenever you are called upon to chair or attend a meeting, make sure up front exactly what is to be covered. Insist on it.

Regardless of what your specialty is, whether you are a secretary, a software engineer, a filing clerk, a delivery person, a CEO, a management trainee, whatever, the same sorts of subject matter barriers have a way of appearing. People tend to react similarly to similar problems, which is why redundant steps, poor time management, and bad habits infest every workplace regardless of task. Removing those will free you to practice your specialty in a more relaxed, creative fashion.

Barrier removal is seldom a one-step process. When a significant obstruction is eliminated, you'll discover new problems that weren't obvious until you removed the first one. Such a pattern might repeat through several phases: the detection and removal of an identified barrier and the exposure of another previously unidentified barrier that suddenly rises to the surface.

If you and everyone else in your company, subject matter experts all, get busy and eliminate the barriers infesting your individual workplaces, you will all have made a real dent in your operational cycle time. But your work will have just begun, because you, your peers, and your bosses are hemmed in also by barriers which exist beyond the realm of your specialty. These are the biggies. Obliterating them may require heavy artillery.

Business Process Barriers

The second category of barriers is interwoven with your company's business processes. Process barriers usually have a profoundly negative impact. To fully appreciate the magnitude of these barriers, you should first have a general idea of the dynamics of corporate business processes. Most companies have two interlocking process loops:

- The *make/market loop* covers every activity from the receipt of an order to the delivery of the requested product or service.

- The *design/development loop* is the time-to-money loop. It covers the steps by which a product or service evolves from a basic concept to a specific, practical, marketable item that makes money.

It should go without saying that these loops contain many subloops, each of which is likewise beset with barriers that retard effective performance. Actually, your specific job is probably a component of one of those subloops. Whereas subject matter barriers respond to individual expertise, business process barriers are tougher to dislodge. They affect many of—perhaps all—the employees in your company.

For the most part, business process barriers are generic, not peculiar to any particular industry. Here are some typical make/market examples:

- Long cycle times cause poor forecasting and fumbling of customer orders.

- Salespeople obtain more orders than can be processed in a responsive manner.

- Salespeople let orders accumulate, then submit them in batches.

- Purchase orders accumulate and then are submitted for sign-offs in batches.

- Equipment is designed to process excessively large lot sizes.

- Shipments between plants are restricted to a weekly basis.
- Problems are defined and without subsequent feedback.
- Excessive overtime, lowered quality standards, and substitute processes are used to get around barriers.
- Office documents are poorly labeled, which leads to administrative confusion.

Similarly, here are some generic design/development barriers:

- Design requirements are forecasted too far ahead of reality because of long cycle times.
- Too many designs are under development at once.
- Designs proceed too far without useful feedback.
- Designers fine-tune their work package before sharing it with others.
- Limited capacity in a company's model shop or drafting section makes for long waits.
- Test-running of prototypes is assigned a low priority by busy manufacturing managers, causing further delay.

A Rogues' Gallery of Process Barriers

Reality Check _____

Subject Company: Silicon Valley microchip manufacturer
Source: Bob Wourms, TGI partner
Situation: Some process barriers stick out like sore thumbs. Bob Wourms had little trouble spotting business process hang-ups right at the start because they were generic.
  The company in question had an important government contract, but its test lab had gotten a bad name when it was unable to provide Uncle Sam with required certification information on its products. Small wonder. Hard times and attrition had damaged the lab's chain of command, and, as Bob recalls, his "team found the group to be in an unmanaged

condition. Employees had essentially continued to perform their jobs autonomously for a year with no one responsible for the big picture."

The first step was to plot the process flow for items requiring a certification test. The sequence, Bob found, began when a receptionist signed for each shipment of "tests," as the items to be certified were called.

WOURMS: She assured me that she logged in each shipment, as long as it arrived during the day shift. Any parts arriving after 4 p.m. were held at the central mailroom until the next working day.... The tests then went across the hall where they were given a computer tracking code. Assignment of the code was critical, she said, to further processing; it was apparently a sophisticated data processing job that took about one week, at which time the tests were returned to her and picked up by the test operators within a day or so to begin qualification. Her work area was neat and orderly with the tests waiting for both computer number assignment and pickup by production in neat stacks.

I crossed the hall to the closed office door of the data processing clerk. He was involved in an intimate conversation with a comely female employee. Incoming lots were stacked three feet deep on his desk, surrounding the computer terminal. Next to the terminal sat a portable color TV tuned to *The Oprah Winfrey Show*. Noting my presence, he turned the TV volume down, and a brief technical discussion ensued, during which I ascertained that obtaining a computerized tracking identification number for each order required 30 to 45 seconds. When I inquired about the lots waiting on his desk, he informed me that Production "didn't need them." I asked how he determined what Production needed. He said that the senior test technician would come and tell him if there was a rush....

Bob talked to the senior technician:

WOURMS: He estimated that the data processing clerk would have to work overtime eight Saturdays to clear the backlog. I dropped in on the clerk that afternoon and told him that the Production group had empty capacity and needed as many lots as he could assign tracking numbers.

The next morning, I went by the clerk's office. He was watching television again. To his credit, he had assigned a tracking number to every lot and had cleared his desk! A one-week process had become a one-day process overnight. No one had ever asked him to assign lot numbers as soon as possible. He said it was "no problem"!

I later discovered that the Manufacturing Information Services group could print out a list of reserved lot numbers which the receptionist could then write directly on the lot traveler without consulting the data processing clerk at all. As soon as she assigned the number, she could put the lot in the Production incoming shelf directly across the hall.

Outcome: By these simple changes, nine days of cycle time were saved! The inventory waiting to be moved to the data clerk, the lots held in the clerk's office, and the lots waiting for pickup by Production were all eliminated, as well as two lot transfers up and down the hallway to the clerk's office.

These results occurred within two days of the program by the simple application of general total cycle time principles. Bob had no previous experience in reliability testing or military certification.

Reality Check

Subject Company: Pressure Systems, Inc., Hampton, VA

Situation: Instead of being regarded as enemies, many serious barriers are treated like 600-pound gorillas. Pressure Systems' baseline cycle time was 20 weeks, and the estimate for entitlement was 5 weeks. One major business process barrier was found in the company's machine shop, where every new order necessitated a time-consuming setup of manufacturing equipment. Once set up, however, such equipment had tremendous productive capacity. Accordingly, after each laborious setup, the shop supervisor produced more than was necessary to fill the order, putting the surplus in inventory to meet future demand. Doing so, he maintained, utilized the equipment up to its capacity and reduced the number of future setups. The trouble with this line of thinking is that it ties up a huge chunk of capital in inventory while on the line overproduction delays the processing of customer orders. As a result, cycle times lengthen.

The cause of Pressure Systems' barrier was the false economy of *letting complex machinery, not customer orders, dictate what and how much to make.* Training was the solution. Several practice runs in setting up the troublesome equipment provided Cycles of Learning about how to simplify the process. Using feedback from each cycle, machine shop people became so speedy that setup times ceased to be a major worry. Gone was the 600-pound gorilla.

Outcome: The company could henceforward manufacture conveniently small lot sizes, which meant much quicker turnaround on customer orders. Moreover, the company could now flush its excess inventory, which provided a needed injection of cash and improved corporate return on assets.

Reality Check

Subject Company: A brand-new software firm specializing in computer-based training

Subject Industry: Computer Software

Situation: The economics of first-pass yield, lot sizes, and customer response are everyday considerations in the manufacturing world, but their impact can be enormous in all types of companies. For the company in question, the talent was superb but the processes all wrong for the custom-designed instructional packages it offered. Here was the process: When a particular client placed an order, a sophisticated training course of about six hours was designed, completed, and presented. There was usually some flaw in the package, however, prompting the customer to reject it. Upon rejection, the product was painstakingly revamped and resubmitted, a process that was financially disastrous. In other words, first-pass yield for this complex, time-consuming operation was poor.

It was pointed out that a six-hour training package was too large a lot size for this all-or-nothing approach. No one in the company had ever thought of such a product in such terms. Nonetheless, the designers were pressed to redefine their task in terms of *small* lot sizes: 20 minutes of instruction per lot.

Conclusion: Since developing small modules was a less complicated, less risky task, the company now could respond faster, improve first-pass yield (thanks to the lot sizes'

manageability and the benefits of rapid feedback), and
eliminate blanket rejection of the final product.

Reality Check _____

Subject Company: A California semiconductor maker

Situation: The company was suffering a major bottleneck
from overlong cycle times in processing personnel requisitions,
capital appropriations, and travel authorizations. The cause
was determined to be the quirky practice of one senior vice
president who had to give his signed approval of such matters.
None of the above were signed during the week *unless
expedited* through his secretary. Otherwise, he let them
accumulate and came in on Saturday to sign.

Conclusion: That single executive preference was causing
many people to spend time expediting their way around him
while others waited with mounting frustration. One person's
unchallenged priorities can easily become a major process
barrier in a company.

---

*Business process barriers are often hidden behind a rationale
that appears superficially sound. But a seemingly innocuous
step may be a major barrier to competitive performance.*

By now, these examples should have you thinking about the
breadth and depth of business process barriers. Following is another eye-opening example of how many different process barriers can feed on each other within a single, well-intentioned
organization.

Reality Check _____

Source: Leon Sipes, TGI partner

Situation: When Leon arrived to crack a cycle time
reduction program, the client company was expanding at a
rate of 25 to 30 percent per year but was riddled with

problems, some of which were the result of growth pressures. Its customer deliveries were late about 60 percent of the time. Its make/market first-pass yield was less than 5 percent. It maintained very high inventories but often did not have the correct stock on hand to fill customer orders. Although it was paying almost $400,000 in annual debt interest, the company had allowed 35 percent of its receivables to get overdue.

Salespeople, though busy, provided no sales forecasts. The chief planner, fresh out of college, issued work orders to Production without knowing if the company had sufficient raw materials on hand. Seeing this, the seasoned production manager simply built to his own plan, accumulating enough extra stock to meet seasonal business surges.

As if all this weren't enough, the purchasing manager was not measured on keeping inventory down. "Consequently," Leon noted, "the raw material warehouse was full and material was stored outside while work orders would frequently be started and have to stop because of insufficient material.... The sales manager frequently interrupted Production with 'hot orders' from key customers.

"To prepare for the heavy season, the plant built inventory, then leased six finished goods warehouses, then added two more, and still had more production and merchandise coming in with no place to put it. Approximately one-third of the raw material was obsolete but still in the warehouses.... Finished goods contained 12 percent inventory that had not moved in over two years. While the company had a central data processing system, the data was not trusted, which resulted in several areas having their own personal computer-based programs, none of which were linked or agreed. Everyone had his own system. The result: low data integrity, low customer delivery percentage.

"The quality control manager was weak and reported to the manufacturing manager. [He was] often used to help load trucks."

Now there was a company with nowhere to go but up. It should come as no surprise that Total Cycle Time techniques worked wonders. A production planning system was devised to enforce discipline throughout the company. The raw material stockpile was reorganized by cutting warehouse space by half and later by two-thirds.

Outcome: With a simple planning system and disciplined data entry, first-pass yield improved rapidly. Productivity improved dramatically, frustration levels fell, and on-time delivery doubled. As Sipes put it, "The company put in place a materials manager responsible for purchasing, planning, and distribution (warehousing, shipping, and receiving). The quality control manager is now a quality *assurance* manager separate from production, and is working on improved processes and procedures to assure quality performance."

All that improvement took place within six months. Incidentally, by reducing inventory by almost 60 percent, the company freed up more than $1.5 million. By reducing its customer service cycle time by half, its annual earnings increased by another $1 million.

Process Barriers: Where Does the Buck Stop?

Barriers that impact *every* sector of an organization may lie in some administrative no-man's land. It may be that no action is ever taken to remove these barriers because they are nobody's business in particular. In fact, barriers of that sort are everybody's business.

Suppose, for example, your paperwork cycle time is one day; that is, you can clear your desk of its daily pile by quitting time. What happens to that work when you route it to its next station? Until it arrives at its intended address, it is at the mercy of interoffice mail. If your company's delivery system is like many, the work you send off will spend a long time in limbo; say two days. It thus takes twice as long to get your completed work to its destination as it did for you to complete it, even if the destination is just two doors down.

It's tough to grapple with obstructions like this one. The time consumed getting paper from one station to another falls into the "white spaces" between people's everyday responsibility. Should you try to do something about it? And if so, what? Isn't life complicated enough without looking for trouble in the mail room or wherever the problem originates? Ask yourself another question: Why should a sheet of paper take two days to find its way into another part of your building? Multiply that lost time by the number of sheets in circulation, and you see that *somebody* ought to do *something* — if you're interested in improving overall performance.

The buck has to stop somewhere. A creative way of overcoming such problems is the cross-functional team: a small task force of interested parties from various parts of the company who are assigned the specific responsibility of fixing a problem. Chances are that when the team removes one business process barrier, the change will expose even more.

Reality Check _____

Subject: Use of Cross-functional Teams
Subject Company: SGS Thomson, France
Subject Industry: Microcircuitry
Source: Harry Pugh, TGI partner
Situation: The Thomson factory in question consisted of three autonomous work centers, each responsible for one of the sequential phases of chip manufacturing: furnaces, photolithography and etching (P&E), and services (additional process steps). Each work center had its own superintendent and self-supporting maintenance team. Theoretically, the system freed superintendents to do the best possible job at their particular manufacturing phase, and Thomson was very proud of its "three factories in one" organization.

The system looked better than it worked, however. As Pugh soon learned, the autonomy of each work center was in fact sapping efficiency.

PUGH: The services engineers reduced the frequency of cleaning of the metal deposition system in order to improve productivity. This caused a notching problem two steps later in the P&E work center.... The P&E engineers, unaware of the change made in services, were trying to solve the notching problem with exotic etching and photoresist processes, resulting in increased rework, more inspections, more scrap, and lower productivity.

That was just one of several cases in which a well-intentioned but unannounced step toward "efficiency" in one area made life miserable for people in another.

PUGH: A source of contamination in a machine used to clean wafers had been found and eliminated by a maintenance technician in furnaces. However, machines of the same type were continuing to generate rework and scrap in the other work centers.

All of which was a high price to pay for each superintendent's autonomy.

Outcome: Because the barriers involved several specialties in all three centers, an across-the-board approach was necessary to unscramble the mess. That was accomplished.

PUGH: Superintendents were encouraged to communicate their problems and successes in a daily meeting, and to take responsibility for problems that originated in their work centers but caused trouble in others. A separate maintenance group was formed spanning all work centers, and it was planned to do the same for process engineering and production.

Put in the terminology of Total Cycle Time, Cycles of Learning (those daily meetings) and a cross-functional approach (those new maintenance, engineering, and production groups) dismantled a pernicious performance problem.

Cultural Barriers

Some of the biggest barriers are cultural, the products of company mindset and myopia. Cultural barriers are well camouflaged, so embedded in a company's infrastructure that they become part of the value system. They are therefore the most difficult to defeat. Their removal, however, has a profound effect on improving competitiveness.

To recall the interoffice mail problem mentioned above: that snag is part of the business process, but it has been around for so many years it has assumed cultural proportions. When such a glitch is pointed out, a managerial disinclination to fix it is cultural. It might be complacency: "The company already runs smoothly and profitably, and changing the mail procedure would be more trouble than it's worth." It could be traditionalism: "We've had this tried-and-true system for years and we're used to it." Perhaps it is individualism: "Everyone is too wrapped up in the challenge of personal assignments to crusade for the company as a whole." Most often, however, the prevailing cultural condition is outright blindness: "*What* mail problem?"!

Although they are rooted in the unique self-image and history of every company, cultural barriers come in generic types. Here are some examples you may recognize:

- The business is viewed as a set of disjointed functions rather than as a business *process* and is measured accordingly.

- Resources are awarded to the dysfunctional elements of the business process.

- Money is spent fighting short-term crises.

- The changing business climate is rationalized because accepting a new cultural mindset is unthinkable.

- Improper measurements are retained because they create an appearance of effective performance.

- Proper measurements are manipulated to create the appearance of effective performance.

- Management fails to hold responsible individuals or teams accountable for failure.

- Managers assume they themselves must spearhead performance improvements.

- Decisions are made by committee.

- In practice, bonus plans don't fit the reward system for which they were designed.

- People are treated differently according to their rank.

The Many Faces of Cultural Barriers

As with business process barriers, there is an understandable but regrettable tendency for individuals at all levels to shrug off cultural barriers on the grounds that such problems are beyond their reach. That's no excuse.

Reality Check _____

Subject Company: GE Subsidiary, Japan
Situation: At this subsidiary, middle managers in finance were asked to complete an elaborate series of data forms sent out by corporate headquarters to all branches. Having distributed the form, the subsidiary's U.S. comptroller was astonished when everyone declined to carry out the assignment. Asking why, she was told that the exercise would add no value to the company's performance. The comptroller duly relayed that message back to the home office, which caused a small uproar.

When the disagreement found its way to the upper levels of GE, top management saw the light.
Outcome: The Japanese employees, whose professional criteria varied from the GE cultural mainstream, had delivered an objective insight on the rest of the company. Their recalcitrance helped inspire a new program at GE called "Work Out," which empowers individuals within the corporation to challenge business process steps that add no value to their jobs. (Eventually, the Japanese managers were persuaded that a few of the forms did indeed add value to GE and duly agreed to complete that select group.)

The cultural inability to see the forest for the trees involves enormously destructive blind spots. Their destructive power is illustrated by the following Reality Check.

Reality Check _____

Subject Company: A Mid-sized Electronics Firm
Subject Process: Purchasing
Source: Vince Donato, TGI partner
Situation: Hank, the company's purchasing agent, had a solid reputation because he was able to procure components at or below last year's prices, a key measurement of a buyer's effectiveness within his company. In other words, the cheaper Hank could buy parts, the higher he rated with his superiors.

One day, Hank was called to a meeting along with managers from other divisions. The company had a big problem: Defective purchased parts were getting through inspection and into the end product, resulting in lower first-pass yield and time-consuming rework. What to do? At the meeting, the quality manager was told to increase the number of inspections, and Hank was told to search diligently for vendors who could supply more reliable components.

Hank was suddenly over a barrel: He was expected to find suppliers whose products wouldn't fail. That he could do, but at a price. Such reliability was costly, and he was also expected to keep his costs at or below last year's, for that was the corporate measure of a good purchasing agent.

Analysis: In reacting to its quality problem, senior management had missed the crux of the issue: its cultural blind spot of making cost the key measurement of a good buyer. As for the immediate problem, its "solution" was actually a substitute process which cost money but did nothing to rectify the underlying fault.

_____

Cultural barriers are usually the hardest to overcome, but their obliteration often produces massive improvements in competitive performance.

_____

Substitute Processes

The archenemy of barrier removal is the substitute process, which can be found at every level in a company. Although it is a way of coping with acknowledged barriers, the substitute process is particularly sinister because, instead of removing the offending barrier, the substitute process provides a detour around it, thereby directing energies away from the basic problem. To make matters worse, such a detour almost invariably requires the application of additional resources. Substitute processes come in all sizes and are often quite innovative. Some are wondrous to behold.

A small but opportune example turned up during a presentation I recently gave in Oslo. A hotel conference room was full of Scandinavian executives who were trying their best to pay attention but were losing the battle to a heating system that made us all swelter. Feeling the effects myself, I called for a break, whereupon several of the attending executives opened doors to the outside, where the temperature was well below freezing. Some even walked outside toward the bank of a frozen lake to relieve their discomfort.

After the break, the doors were again closed and, as before, the temperature inevitably started to climb. We repeated this process many times. As distracting as it was, it at least provided an opportunity for instruction. "Here," I said, "is an example of a substitute process. Because the building's climate control is fixed elsewhere, our performance here is suffering. All we can do to get around the problem is to let in the winter from outside. Better to fix the basic process than waste time working around it." One of the people in the room contacted the hotel management, and we at least obtained a satisfactory business process for the remainder of the meeting.

Reality Check _____

Subject: Trouble, Even in Paradise
Subject Company: Thomas Group Inc.
Subject Industry: Performance Improvement
Situation: A few months ago, a substitute process was exposed right in my own backyard. All our partners are

prodigious business travelers, and our travel arrangements had customarily been arranged by members of the office secretarial pool using an outside travel agency. This complicated, time-consuming method often required several callbacks and rearrangements before the right tickets could be issued. It also worked a hardship on our busy support staff. One partner privately calculated that it took him an average of four phone calls of up to five minutes each, with 50 percent rework, to get a single ticket, which amounted to a pretty long cycle time and poor first-pass yield for any company, much less us. Accordingly, he and others resorted to a substitute process. When he needed to travel, he called a travel agent directly, bypassing all the bureaucracy and rework and completing his arrangements on one pass. Well and good, except that the faulty system stayed in place, more confused than ever by the vigilante use of multiple agents. Eventually, the in-house barrier and the substitute process drew our attention, and action was taken. We now have two professional travel agents in house and an 800 number available to partners on the road.

Reality Check

Subject Industry: Engine manufacture

Situation: A recent visit to a major manufacturing customer revealed the other end of the substitute process spectrum. Theoretically, this customer's stock in trade is a series of standard engines, and its manufacturing line, inherited from a high-volume standard engine plant, is set up according to that tradition. Surprisingly, however, less than half of the company's customers order a "standard" engine. The products are in fact mostly custom. To shepherd custom orders through the noncustom business process, company managers had devised substitute processes which collectively constituted an unbelievably intricate pipeline of paperwork and irregular procedures that handled more engines than the company's legitimate manufacturing process. In reality, these substitute processes were the company's system, not the established process to which people paid lip service. Yet the company had not taken adequate steps to reconcile the situation. When, during a review, this matter, so obvious to outsiders, was mentioned, a lot of lights came on in executive eyes.

Substitute processes aren't necessarily makeshift. Some can be purchased outright as prescribed "solutions," the packaged, short-lived, fad-of-the-year miracle cures that promise to improve U.S. business performance but seldom deliver any permanent results. A few of these are substitute processes pure and simple.

Several years ago, hundreds of companies embraced the concept of matrix management, seeking to break through managerial logjams that were paralyzing their conventional, vertical chain of command. Matrix management overlaid a permanent horizontal structure on the vertical. Managers were reshuffled into an additional set of power groupings to oversee special objectives.

Matrix management by and large is proving too complicated, confusing, and unwieldy to last. Worse, it is a *substitute process*. Any company whose structure is so ineffective as to require alternatives is a company with fundamental problems—barriers to effective performance—that should be eliminated, not plastered over. Nonetheless, some of the United States' largest corporations are still deeply involved with matrix management. The fact that top brass at these companies embrace so colossal a substitute process dramatizes the power of cultural myopia.

Why are substitute processes so numerous? The answer is that they are the instinctual way for subject matter experts to counteract problems in the overall business process. When a problem arises, the average person reacts by adding resources. In a temporary emergency, substitute processes may be a legitimate way to tide an organization over, but only until it rids itself of its underlying business process barrier.

Substitute Processes: Where Does the Buck Stop?

The fact that substitute processes are honestly come by does not, however, relieve people in middle and lower ranks of the responsibility to spot and remove them. It does not re-

lieve you from that responsibility. Before your mindset
prompts you to say that substitute processes are beyond your
power, consider the following situation.

Reality Check _____

Subject Process: Purchasing
Situation: Stu Frank, a clerk in the delivery dock of a
large company, was repeatedly inconvenienced. When
goods arrived at the dock, he could not always get the
computerized purchasing system to yield a copy of its
purchase order so he could match it with the incoming
goods. Were such mystery arrivals legitimate or mistakes?
Rather than let them pile up, Stu invented an expedient: he
would fax the vendors, claiming he needed "a verification,"
and prevail upon each to send a copy of the purchase order.
Here was a substitute process in the making. Far from
attacking his company's faulty record system, Stu was
backhandedly endorsing it.
   He stuck with this approach for a while because he was
convinced there was nothing a mere clerk could do to
revamp a software system devised by higher-ups. But it was
also of course an imposition upon vendors, and it made Stu
look like a stumblebum. Finally, his professional pride got
the better of him, so he screwed up his courage and made a
cafeteria lunch date with Mary Malloy, his company's chief
systems planner.
Outcome: When he told the story of the elusive purchase
orders, it was news to Mary, who promptly put down her
sandwich, scribbled a few lines in a pocket notebook, and
assured Stu it would be a simple matter to fix. She even
thanked our hero for having the gumption to bring the
hidden problem to her attention.
Analysis: There are two morals to this tale. The first is that a
substitute process complicates life without eliminating barriers.
The second is that it pays to exceed your authority when you
spot a "varmint." Suppose, however, that Mary had gotten on
her high horse and dismissed the complaint? Even a complete
brush-off would be a small price for Stu to pay for the
satisfaction of having done the right thing.

Killing snakes is everybody's business. There are probably some snakes that only you can spot.

Another cultural substitute process is the common tendency to confuse actions with results.

Reality Check

Subject Industry: Manufacturing

Situation: A thorough assessment of a huge manufacturing firm revealed that it was riddled with performance barriers. The situation was made clear to the corporate chairman, but instead of directing the accountable vice presidents to remove the barriers forthwith, he initiated his own elaborate "fact-finding study" to determine the hows and whys of the company's deterioration. No barrier removal occurred while this study was in process, but top brass felt they could relax because some "action was being taken." The fact that the action was nothing more than a data-loaded research project and not a step to ease the company's strain seemed wasted on everyone except an outsider.

Conclusion: Stu Frank's purchase order problem was a business process barrier that the right subject matter expert could fix. Such substitute processes as the engine company's unofficial pipeline or fact-finding approaches to "taking action" have deeper roots.

- *When it comes to barrier removal, talking and action are two different things.*
- *Action that fails to remove barriers is not effective action.*
- *Action, when chosen, should add value to the company.*

Barrier Circles

The mixture of subject matter, business process, and cultural barriers can be visualized as a set of circles within circles, all of which surround the tasks at hand and restrain effective performance. Let's take a typical make/market example, in which the smallest business process circle represents a basic unit such as a clerk in a company's order entry department. The outer edge of that clerk's little circle touches the inner edge of a larger circle representing the entire order entry department (Figure 5.1). Order entry is a make/market subloop with its own set of process barriers. The order entry circle's outer rim touches the inner rim of the largest circle, one which envelops the entire make/market process and bedevils top management. You may be a long way from your CEO in the chain of command, but in terms of barrier circles, you're just a few ripples away from the top. And because the barri-

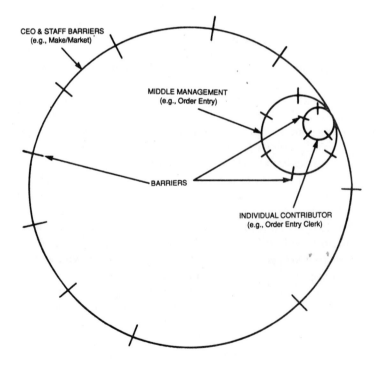

Figure 5.1. Barrier Circles.

ers of adjoining circles exert a negative influence that can be felt throughout the entire process loop, the barriers you leave untended affect your CEO's performance.

- *Subject matter, business process, and cultural barriers are inherent to every company. There are no exceptions.*
- *In every category, barriers are primarily generic.*
- *Substitute processes exist at every level and are often willingly embraced as solutions, not obstructions.*
- *Barriers are not the exclusive territory of top management. They occur at every level, right down to the individual contributor.*

Time's A-Wasting

Perhaps all this talk about barriers and substitute processes sounds a bit irrelevant to you. From where you sit, it may not seem as though your company fits the examples and generalizations provided here. But appearances can be deceiving. Unless your company lives and breathes short-cycle-time culture and exploits Cycles of Learning, it is certain that your own professional life operates below its entitlement.

The gap between baseline and entitlement holds the opportunity for your company's survival and your professional well-being. At entitlement, life on the job is exciting, because the daily frustrations, busywork, slowdowns, and the lack of purpose will have vanished. Freed from barriers and burdens that you probably couldn't see for looking, you won't be working harder, just more effectively.

As we have seen, the performance gap between baseline and entitlement is seldom a question of outright neglect or incompetence. Companies with the best of intentions unwittingly labor under bad habits, red tape, obsolete methods, false assumptions, incorrect measurements, and contradictory procedures, almost all of which they have come by honestly. But when the time comes for change, they are tempted to add steps, spend more money, hire more people, and buy more equipment instead of improving the performance of the resources on hand. The result? *More* performance barriers and *longer* customer service cycle times.

Time, of course, is what the competitiveness crisis is all about. Windows of opportunity are growing ever shorter as the pace of business accelerates. If your competition can respond to customers' needs more quickly and flexibly, you can guess who's going to inherit your business. Don't let that happen.

Because so many of your company's business process and cultural barriers may be hard to identify, it takes more than determination and a keen eye to get rid of them. Your company's two best tools for barrier removal are Cycles of Learning and coaching.

Exposing Barriers Through Cycles of Learning

Everyone learns from experience in an informal manner. A few are even able to reach their entitlement on their own—but only a few.

Not many companies or employees bother to provide themselves with a formal mechanism for learning from experience, which these days is as dangerous as fighting a war without an air force. Instead, many corporate leaders institute cosmetic measures that lull them into a false sense of security. I recently listened to a glowing tale of a company's newly instituted "open door policy," in which all executives theoretically make themselves accessible to all employees. Wishful thinking, I thought. Another company bragged about its "idea program," which was little more than the placement of suggestion boxes here and there throughout the corporate premises. Who are these managers kidding? Those two companies are suffering from acute cultural myopia.

Every loop or subloop of a business must maintain a permanent, formal mechanism which analyzes the performance of each completed cycle of activity and defines refinements for the next. The key measurements for every feedback mechanism in every Cycle of Learning are cycle time, reduction of actions in process, and first-pass yield. How long did the task take to complete (and why), how much was the activity in process reduced (and how), and how much activity was done right the first time (and why)?

Every Cycle of Learning and feedback mechanism should also include a forcing function to motivate individuals to accept and apply the lessons of experience. In other words, employee performance should be evaluated according to each individual's cycle time and first-pass yield.

Coaching by Outsiders: Helping the Blind to See

How can a company root out the high-leverage business process and cultural barriers that are entwined with its infrastructure? One way is to develop an information system that actively solicits employee and customer feedback. Getting wind of problems before they grow into lawsuits, strikes, and lost clientele will eliminate some blind spots.

But not all. Customers may be well-enough informed to offer constructive criticism, but they are hardly equipped to know where the barriers lie within your company's business process or culture. And when it comes to cultural barriers, your own people are at a distinct disadvantage. The most dutiful internal teams and task forces cannot achieve the perspective necessary to expose the most subtle (and often most pernicious) barriers. That is why it may be worthwhile for your company to seek experienced outside assistance.

It is, of course, true that no group of problem solvers possesses the subject matter expertise required to correct the immediate glitches in your particular workspace. You are best equipped to do that. The outsider's stock in trade is spotting business process and cultural hang-ups, areas where subject matter expertise can actually be a handicap. Sometimes, the less subject matter expertise an outsider possesses, the better.

Companies that have made some progress toward entitlement but have run out of momentum short of the goal sometimes have to seek outside assistance. Such a circumstance invariably involves cultural myopia. Blinded to the possibility that certain practices don't work or are leading the company in the wrong direction, managers insist on retaining useless, resource-hungry, misleading measurements simply because they've been in force for 20 years or so.

In one troubled firm, growth itself was the sacred measurement that had hypnotized management. That company, its managers proudly claimed, was growing 10 percent per year. Well and good, but its market was growing by 20 percent. In the present position, to regain its one-time share of the market, growth should be up 30 percent!

Barrier Removal Is Frustration Removal

The entire process of barrier removal, especially the effort that involves business process and cultural roadblocks, is a complicated, multilayered process. Two final points should be emphasized:

1. There are more barriers than you realize. As the ones closest to the surface of everyday activity disappear, others, hidden by that first layer, will surface. The streamlining process may proceed in stages.

2. Every barrier removed constitutes one less non-value-added hurdle for you to deal with in accomplishing your task. Consequently, you will be performing more effectively without having to increase the pace of your work, enabling you to take on more tasks and increase your value to the company.

From Mindset to Mechanics

By now, you have probably acquired a proper respect for the size and complexity of the barrier problem, which is part of the time warrior's mindset. Mindset, however, must be fortified with effective weapons.

Three R's and Five I's

Accelerating Improvement:
The Three R's

Competitiveness embraces three mutually dependent factors which can be referred to as the *Three R's*. Every self-respecting time warrior must come to terms with these Three R's and use them to gauge personal and organizational effectiveness. If you or your company command all three—and only if you command *all three*—you are performing at entitlement and are truly competitive.

The Three R's are

- Responsiveness (the quicker the better)
- Results (the quicker the better)
- Resources (the more effectively used the better)

The First R: Responsiveness

Responsiveness is the degree to which a business can meet its customers' needs on time, using minimal resources. "On time" means the ability to provide customers with the goods or services requested on or before a mutually agreeable deadline. Timely response is becoming more of a trademark of competitiveness with each passing week. If you cannot meet your customers' schedules, someone who can will soon take your place.

By way of illustration, let's assume you are in manufacturing. If you have trouble responding, it is because your make/

113

market cycle time is too long. Make/market cycle time is the time it takes to enter an order, forecast, schedule, purchase material, receive and stock it, make the required goods, ship, and collect payment. (Each of these activities is of course a make/market subloop with its own cycle time.) To provide proper customer service, the make/market loop's cycle time must be shorter than the elapsed time from the point at which an order was received to the point when it is deliverable. To bring new products to market before the competition, your design/development loop's cycle time — the time needed to conceive, design a new product and bring it to cost-effective production — must be the shortest in the business. If it's not, someone else's product will get the drop on yours.

Short cycle times are thus crucial to winning the time war; they provide one of the most important measurements of how you are doing. Nonetheless, most companies do not recognize that long cycle times are to blame for poor response. More often, you hear:

"Our forecasting is poor!" Managers blame their problems on insufficient or incompetent forecasting. They react by adding more forecasters and more inventory. Those are exactly the wrong tactics for winning the time war. It wastes time and money because poor forecasting is seldom to blame. The real problem is overlong cycle times, which require forecasters to look too far into the future.

When cycle times are too long, beefing up the forecasting function is a substitute process that masks the real problem.

"We need to get our processes under control!" Managers believe that they could respond more effectively if additional controls were added. More inspections, sign-offs, meetings, and paperwork would keep the actions in process from getting out of hand, right? Wrong.

Long cycle time processes are inherently unpredictable. There are too many barriers out there, and adding steps will worsen the problem.

"We need to add resources to keep up with orders!" Almost every manager sinking under the weight of long cycle times thinks that his or her life would be easier if there were more people, more equipment, or more money on hand to cope with the changing times.

Adding resources when performance is at baseline throws good money after bad. Cutting cycle times requires no new resources.

"We need to keep our customers from changing their orders so much!" When orders are revised, it makes forecasters' and managers' lives miserable. To forestall such changes, managers often expend time and effort on controlling their customers. That way, changes in schedule, mix, specifications, and price will not spoil the forecast. At the root of such snarls, however, are long cycle times which extend the period in which customers might change their minds.

When cycle times are reduced, the number of change requests diminishes.

Responsiveness is crucial to competitiveness. Measure yourself and your company by your ability to provide timely response.

Poor responsiveness is caused by long cycle time.

Timely, precise response is achieved by shortening cycle time.

The Second R: Results

Time is of the essence in the race for corporate survival. The results you seek include:

- Improved responsiveness
- Higher quality
- Better productivity
- Increased profits
- Greater return on assets
- Lower costs.

All can be accelerated by Cycles of Learning. If you're involved in a Total Cycle Time effort, you'll be accelerating the pace of your improvement that way. If not, you are probably hearing the following litany:

> ***"Our improvements seem to take so long!"*** Of course they do, if your actions in process are too numerous and if you're not using Cycles of Learning. Improvements are slowed by failure to reduce actions in process, to remove resources applied to meaningless, non-value-added steps, and to apply the lessons of experience.

Making improvements does not involve good guessing. It involves objective analysis of your past performance.

> ***"Adding resources will accelerate our results!"*** This is a self-deceiving "solution." On the defensive, too many managers blame their problems on shorthandedness. But if managers are not using Cycles of Learning, they're not using existing resources effectively. Adding more resources just adds to the problem.

Bear in mind that these generalizations apply to any and every business. Use of the manufacturing analogy is for the sake of convenience and should not be taken to mean that

Total Cycle Time is for manufacturers only. Far from it. Problem solving in any business requires that you complete the process, evaluate the results, and feed creative solutions back into the process.

If you cut cycle times by reducing your actions in process, you have more opportunities to try, test, modify, and learn.

The more complex the process, the more positive the impact of Cycles of Learning.

The Third R: Resources

Although getting by on minimal resources is a motherhood issue with time warriors, the urge to add resources is very powerful when a crisis pops up. Many problems are in fact a function of having too many, not too few, resources. On the road to entitlement, resources are scrutinized with an eye to doing more with what's available rather than what might be added.

The root of the misuse of resources is long cycle times, which give rise to the following complaints:

"We need more inventory so we can fill those hurry-up orders!" When customers appear to be impatient, or if they frequently change their orders, many troubled companies respond by stockpiling inventory so that they can fill any and every order. Managers, furthermore, are often all too willing to play this game because they are compensated according to the size of the resources they manage. Adding inventory, alas, is a strategic mistake.

Besides tying up assets, large inventories are a cover-up for a problem. They mask poor response times and the inability to adjust the mix when a customer revises an order.

Reality Check _____

Subject Company: A high-tech manufacturer in California
Situation: This company became alarmed when its fortunes
nosedived. During an assessment, the top managers were
asked to describe the company's areas of excellence.
"Performance to schedule," was the reply. "Ours is superior to
all competitors'! We deliver our products to customers
precisely at the promised time and in the proper mix." That
sounded good, but the method of achieving performance to
schedule was to maintain an inventory about twice the size of
competitors' and to accept only orders with long lead times.

   Because its cycle times were too long and getting longer, the
only way the company could perform to schedule was by
stockpiling inventory with which to meet demand, a perfect
example of performance-at-any-cost mindset.

Conclusion: A year later, when it had gotten its
make/market cycle time under control, the same company was
able to retain its performance to schedule without the
ponderous inventory, and profitability picked up accordingly.

Reality Check _____

Subject Company: Texas Instruments
Source: Doug Connor, TGI partner
Situation: During an effort to reduce dock-to-stock cycle
time at a Texas Instruments facility, Doug Connor was
intrigued by the plant's apparent policy of holding work in
process in lots of 1500. He wondered what was magic about
that number. After hours of fruitless interviews and data
analysis, he took a quick look around and found the answer:
Lots of 1500 were exactly the right size to fill the plant's
available storage space. "As work in process was reduced via
the traditional Five I's process," said Doug, "shelf space was
removed to only hold entitlement work in process: 250."

Reality Check _____

Subject Company: Coleman Outdoor Products, Wichita,
Kansas

Source: Bonnie Sloan, TGI partner

Situation: As at many companies, the obsession with inventory had taken on cultural proportions at Coleman. Bonnie recalled that the company's Thermal Productions Division possessed an "enormous warehouse of finished goods, and overhead catwalks throughout the huge factory filled with work in process. Some finished goods had six or seven labels on top of each other for yearly promotional updates. A motorized vehicle was used to traverse the finished goods area.

"All barriers were masked with inventory. The overhead inventories increased cycle time and reduced opportunities for Cycles of Learning." The divisional manager, however, became a convert to the new culture and set a decisive example. Accordingly, the Thermal Productions manager knew he had to cut his inventory.

Outcome: According to Bonnie, he decided the only way to stop storing inventory was to eliminate the overhead storage areas. He did so by applying a blowtorch to the catwalks. The division used feedback loops to cut cycle times and improve first-pass yield. Thermal Productions' example inspired other managers to get started and drew favorable attention from senior management. As Bonnie put it, "sometimes it takes a blowtorch to change a strong culture."

Inventory is a more serious problem than your company probably realizes because conventional bookkeeping does not account for invisible inventory. An example of invisible inventory is the cash tied up (though expensed) in activities in progress such as designs under way, cost-reduction programs, and development. Invisible inventory is usually substantial. If your company spends 10 percent of annual sales on development (a typical figure) and your development cycle time is three years, the cash tied up in invisible inventory amounts to 30 percent of annual sales!

Stockpiling inventory is a costly substitute process that denies the fundamental problem: overlong cycle times.

Large quantities of visible and invisible inventory are signs of a noncompetitive operation.

"We need to automate to be competitive!" In this case, the perception is that more computerized information will provide a tactical advantage. But automating long-cycle-time, barrier-laden processes actually entrenches them further and increases overhead to boot. There may be some appearance of improved performance, but real competitiveness will be undermined by the expensive, misapplied hardware and software.

Reality Check

Subject Industry: Manufacturing/Sales

Situation: A manufacturing company was experiencing overlong order entry cycle times among its field sales force. To speed up the paperwork, a plan was afoot to invest in sophisticated software and equip every salesperson with a laptop computer. The tab for the proposed software and laptops was several million dollars, and the anticipated time to get the plan in place was upward of two years.

Outcome: Upon reconsidering the problem, management elected to remove existing barriers instead. In a matter of months, the order entry process was close to the desired performance level without the addition of a single laptop or software package.

Entitlement is by definition achievable without adding new resources.

"We could improve performance by installing new resources early!" This misperception can occur even during a drive for Total Cycle Time. It is based upon the notion that adding resources early enough will guarantee the output desired. The root of this problem is again long cycle times. For example, if a design process takes three years, its first steps must be staffed three years in advance of the anticipated output. If, however, cycle times were reduced by two-thirds (which is typical), the early steps would require only a year's advance notice.

Don't service long cycle times by asking for more resources. Shorten the cycle times.

"We'd do better if upper management stopped saying no to our requests!" Not necessarily, especially if upper management has gotten the bug to reduce cycle times. Is it possible that top brass sees the trap of adding resources before reaching entitlement?

When counseling senior management on Total Cycle Time, I borrow a phrase from the former first lady's antidrug campaign: "Just say no." However inadequate that slogan may have been in its original context, it is made to order for management during the move to Total Cycle Time.

Unless your company has arrived at its entitlement, whatever improvement you seek through added resources is achievable through the alternative of barrier removal. Make it happen.

Optimizing Existing Resources Is Crucial to Competitiveness

Some of the United States' most dangerous competitors—Pacific Rim companies—have achieved responsiveness through high inventories and the massing of resources. With few exceptions, they are hooked on the availability of low-cost capital and cheap labor through which they maintain their market position *despite* long cycle times. This mindset is cultural in the largest sense, a product of Asian history and societal tradition. In the United States, where capital and labor do not come cheap, there is absolutely no point in trying to beat Asia at its own game. However, there is an enormous opportunity to *outflank* those competitors by combining U.S. ingenuity with Cycles of

Learning, by eliminating resource-hungry barriers, and by slashing response times.

When it comes to resources, time warriors at all levels must discard the let's-add-resources mentality in exchange for the Total Cycle Time mindset.

Total Cycle Time and the Three R's

Total Cycle Time drives the Three R's of competitiveness:

- Total Cycle Time permits you to respond to customers' needs rapidly, flexibly, and economically by shortening your cycle times.

- Total Cycle Time permits you to accelerate the results you require through Cycles of Learning.

- Total Cycle Time permits you to get the most out of your resources by simplifying your business processes and eliminating substitute processes.

The relationship of Total Cycle Time to the Three R's is easy to grasp. In fact, all of the new mindset is easy to grasp in principle. Putting the mindset into place is much harder and involves another process, the Five I's.

The Five I's: Getting from Here to There

Getting you and your company to entitlement is a multiphase process, each phase of which is essential for longstanding success. I have already likened the adoption of Total Cycle Time to the decision to go on a sensible diet, the kind that promises permanent benefits if you don't backslide. The weight loss analogy is all too familiar to me because I have been through such a program. Inasmuch as more than half of U.S. adults are on a diet of some sort at the time of this writing, the analogy may have personal meaning to you, too.

A couple of years ago, during my annual physical examination, my doctor ordered me to shed a few pounds. His reasons were so sound that I could hardly argue, and he was so reassuring that I got enthusiastic about the prospect. Because quick results were in keeping with my short-cycle-time mindset, I elected to try a medically supervised crash program. I plunged in, weighing myself every two days. Each time I stepped on the scale and the statistical feedback stared up at me, I completed another Cycle of Learning. It was very gratifying: I was shedding a pound a day. My inspiration mounted.

If you've ever been down this road yourself, you know what happened next. A few weeks into the program, my inspiration began to sag. For one thing, the novelty had worn off; for another, my pound-a-day momentum ceased. My body had apparently used its own Cycles of Learning to become more efficient on less food, so, as my metabolic rate slowed down, my progress did likewise. This was turning out to be harder than I thought! By that time, however, I was used to the regimen, so I swallowed my day-to-day discouragement and saw the program through to the end. Eventually, I reached my target weight.

Taking off weight can be tough, but keeping it off is even tougher. With that in mind, I had been coached during the program about the necessity of changing my attitude about food and adopting a new mindset for keeps. I was *not* to assume that once I'd reached my entitled goal, I could resume the dining habits that had gotten me into trouble in the first place. My days of seductive sauces and syrupy desserts were over, period. In other words, the diet was accompanied by behavior modification or, to use my phrase, a culture change. Sure enough, when I completed the regimen, I had gained a healthy mindset to complement my slimmer figure.

None of this was easy, mind you. Inspiration could carry me just so far. Beyond that point, acquired discipline and new mindset took over. Behavior modification is seldom absolute, however, and to this day, when I'm in my favorite restaurant, it's not easy to stay sensible when the dessert cart rolls by.

Putting Total Cycle Time in place is exactly like sensible weight loss and involves a multipart process called the *Five I's*. The components are

- Inspiration (the call to action)
- Identification (determining what is possible)
- Information (learning needed new approaches)
- Implementation (making the new approaches work)
- Internalization (anchoring the new culture).

Although the Five I's begin with Inspiration and end with Internalization, the process is *not* sequential. The various components will always overlap.

If *all* these phases are properly installed, the Five I's will get you to entitlement and keep you there. If one or more phases is missing, however, the results will likewise be partial and temporary.

The First I: Inspiration

As with going on a diet, the first step toward positive behavior modification is to get motivated. People are inspired to improve if they believe the performance goal is desirable and realistic and the methodology reasonable. To a large extent, this book is dedicated to that first I, Inspiration. Its intent is to motivate you by demonstrating the urgency and benefits of becoming a time warrior.

The world of business draws its inspiration from two sources: preachers and practitioners. Some of the best-known business preachers are communicators who can sell a concept but cannot supply a process by which to achieve it. They are like the quick-buck artists who, every week or so it seems, come out with another miracle diet. Enough is enough. You don't have time to waste on a series of not-so-miraculous miracle cures and neither does your company.

The Inspiration phase is a bit more important than it may sound at first. It is not a pep rally, because cultural change does not take place in a rah-rah atmosphere. All levels of the organization must want to change, and the methods used to inspire each level must be adjusted accordingly.

When the time warrior concept spreads to the company as a whole, Inspiration should flow from the top down. It's important to make sure that senior managers have become time warriors (time generals, actually) before moving down the line to enlist management teams, middle managers, and individual contributors. CEOs and senior managers are, as a rule, not difficult to inspire, probably because they are used to thinking strategically and do not feel threatened by the many changes required by Total Cycle Time. Sometimes all it takes is chemistry.

Reality Check _____

Subject Company: Fairchild semiconductor plant, Portland, Maine
Source: Alex Young, TGI President
Situation: Key people who reject the time warrior concept at the start cannot be counted on to pass inspiration downstream. At Fairchild's Portland plant, for example, cycle time facilitator Alex Young was virtually stonewalled. Senior management had endorsed a proposal to shorten cycle times, yet when assessment of the design group began, the manager in charge was not to be found. While Alex was talking with a properly inspired subordinate, the telephone rang. It was the boss, who from his hiding place told the subordinate to clam up and ordered Alex out of the building! Obviously, the Five I's had an uphill battle in that case.

Reality Check _____

Subject Company: Pressure Systems, Inc.

Source: Doug Connor, TGI partner

Situation: The enthusiasm of this company's CEO and operational VP was expressive and abundant. With that kind of high-level support, what could go wrong? Plenty. PSI was committed to a "nonassertive management approach" in which it was considered bad form for top dogs to lean heavily on subordinates. Nobody on top was going to push Total Cycle Time down the PSI chain of command, so the program got off to a slow start.

One way to inspire lukewarm employees, however, is to provide a tangible link between their individual efforts and the results desired. To this end, PSI instituted a program in which each of its 100 employees would receive a bonus based upon improved profits. It worked wonders.

CONNOR: When line operators started to receive a monthly bonus, their inspiration level improved immediately. For example, two machine operators asked if they could haul away cleared timbers from the site to avoid paying money to a contractor, and a first shift operator noticed that shop lights were left on at night even though no one was working and mentioned that to the TCT team as a barrier. Problem resolved.

Outcome: Incentive-based bonuses are one of the most inspirational ways to effect changes of mindset.

What is the situation where you work? Because Inspiration is a responsibility of senior management, it will be necessary to get top brass involved to secure a general move to entitlement. Your part in that process is to share your improved results with your peers and your boss so that the new mindset moves up the ladder. Nobody expects one warrior to win a war, but you can make an effective start.

As with a weight loss program, that original burst of enthusiasm won't carry you along singlehandedly once the novelty wears off and the hard work begins. By then, you must be nurtured by the potential results you are identifying and by training that will give you the tools to reach your goal. Those are the next two of the Five I's.

Inspiration is not a matter of waving banners and wearing badges with encouraging slogans. Inspiration is instead a matter of gut-level acceptance of the logic, methodology, and potential of Total Cycle Time.

Inspiration must flow from the top down to be fully effective. If you are pioneering the new mindset, remember that you must get people higher up involved. But senior advocacy does not guarantee that everyone down the line accepts the new mindset. To some, it's too good to be true; to others, it's a threat to their comfortable routine. Therefore, champions are needed at all levels. Although Inspiration is the first of the I's, it cannot cease as other phases begin.

The Second I: Identification

In Chapter 4, you determined your current performance (baseline) and realizable performance (entitlement) levels. When your company elects Total Cycle Time, it must do likewise for every process loop and subloop, using a similar but more complex process, Identification, the second I in the series. The Identification phase adds substance to Inspiration by providing hard figures on what has been achieved and what is achievable. Theoretically, once your company has identified its baseline and entitlement, the order of action is Information (training), Implementation (barrier identification and removal), and Internalization (solidifying the change to continuous improvement).

But life does not always proceed according to theory. Although each of the Five I's must be covered in any successful Total Cycle Time effort, nothing is stopping you from taking immediate action (Implementation) if you are inspired to do so and know where to act. As you saw in Chapter 5, that was how Bob Wourms knocked nine days off one of his client's cycle time after two days on the job. And when, during my inspection of that huge manufacturing company, the sight of its bizarre fleet of golf carts hit me between the eyes, I recognized a process glitch that needed to be attacked forthwith—no need to wait for the logical process of the Five I's to play themselves out. Conspicuous barriers are like low-hanging fruit, ripe for easy picking.

Reality Check _____

Subject Company: Philips/Signetics
Subject Industry: Semiconductors
Source: Bruce Hanson, TGI partner
Situation: Bruce Hanson led a cross-functional team trying to identify entitlement for Signetics' design/development cycle. Given the enormous numbers of semiconductors Signetics supplies to industry, timely design can make the difference between being the business leader or an also-ran. But the company was working on too many products at once and prolonging the agony of each. To determine the design/development loop's entitlement, the team decided to negotiate with each of the company's six product line management teams, seeking to prioritize designs and, if possible, limit their number.

"But," as Bruce recalled, "the members had little or no understanding about how low first-pass yield contributes to long cycle times due to rework, little or no realization of the effect actions in process have on cycle times, and a strong belief—a cultural barrier—that more resources were needed to shorten design/development cycle time. There were already several hours of team time invested in analysis and review of the existing process and the baseline values for each subprocess. The team had prepared their case for their entitlement goals and presented it to us....It showed about a 10 percent improvement, and nearly all was to come out of other groups [than Design]....I told them they would need to be much more aggressive to achieve the kind of competitiveness found in the industry. Further, that trying to fully understand how to accomplish big changes now was not possible. For technical and analytical type people, this kind of faith in a strange new methodology was very difficult."

Bruce finally made "the impact of high actions in process more clear by asking how many engineers could be productively used on one project. Typically, they assigned only one. This group agreed that three or four could be used—if they were able to hire them! I said, 'Suppose you hired them; then what would be the improvement in the Design subprocess?'

"Their answer was 'a reduction of over 40 percent.' When combined with some improved first-pass yield assumptions, the total improvement was over 50 percent.

"I said, 'That is entitlement!' They said, 'No new resources are allowed.' I said, 'Then cancel low-priority projects and staff the high-priority ones.'"

Outcome: "There was a long, stunned silence as the real meaning of entitlement was absorbed. This scenario, with variations, was repeated several times and resulted in rather competitive design/development goals for entitlement."

Furthermore, this exercise in Identification proved downright inspirational to some team members, for whom the multiplicity of stalled projects had meant added paperwork and lowered morale. After coaching that team, Bruce affirmed that during Identification, people "must at least see a 'plausibility' on a personal level, of the entitlement goals. Otherwise, there will be no ownership for the needed results."

The Identification phase is where the opportunities for you or your company to improve performance are quantified, making baseline and entitlement more real.

Outside expertise will make Identification more precise by eliminating the self-deception and data rationalization that inevitably cloud internal studies. If you want objectivity, go outside.

The Third I: Information

Reality Check _____

Subject Company: Harris Semiconductor, Palm Bay, Florida
Situation: An objective assessment convinced me that Harris had room for dramatic performance improvement. The rationale was given in a report to Harris, along with recommendations about how to proceed. Harris's people seemed inspired to raise the time warrior banner and slash their cycle times. After a game effort, they stopped dead, far short of entitlement, and they called me back to determine why.
Analysis: Although Harris employees were motivated, they lacked the necessary skills to make war on the company's longstanding barriers. A training program was the answer to overcoming the deficiency. Since that time, I have included the Information phase as part of the Total Cycle Time package.

To return to the Signetics case, one of the first steps was to give the company's manufacturing managers a crash course in Total Cycle Time implementation. Inspired, instructed, and determined to exploit Cycles of Learning, those managers returned home to make things happen. But things didn't happen. The trouble, they found, was that subordinates lacked the skills to use high-low diagnostics (the technique of analyzing best- and worst-case performance), without which they could not exploit Cycles of Learning.

Time warriors need effective weapons. Accordingly, the lower-level people were pumped full of the requisite know-how, and the Implementation phase picked up momentum.

The skills shortfall shows itself differently in different workplaces, and it is pointless to plunge into a companywide entitlement quest without the right training. It is also expecting too much for a company to get wisdom about what sort of training is necessary before the actual need arises. The Information phase, therefore, is another area in which objectivity can be crucial.

Training is traditionally viewed as a preface to action. In other words, it is assumed that people should be given the skills necessary to grapple with a problem before attacking it.

Employers are forever saying that employees need hands-on training before they try to implement change. That kind of training won't work. You can only transfer hands-on skills when people know what they're expected to accomplish. Furthermore, when they know what's expected of them, they are likely to listen very closely to the training.

The need for training is almost always in generic rather than subject matter areas. Most often, people need to acquire skills to:

- Map and analyze the business process
- Work effectively as a team
- Reduce cycle times
- Use Cycles of Learning effectively
- Identify and remove barriers.

You can see that training and doing go hand in hand. Needed skill sets should be acquired concurrently with actual barrier removal (Implementation).

If, during your own attempt to cut personal cycle time, you realize that you lack the essential know-how to attack barriers, by all means ask your boss for some training. If you are up against process barriers, it's a cinch that you are not alone and that training would make a big difference with your peers as well.

Information, the third of the Five I's, begins shortly after Identification and initial barrier removal have exposed training needs. Information proceeds parallel with Implementation.

The Fourth I: Implementation

When properly motivated people apply themselves to cutting cycle times, the organized thrust to entitlement—Implementation—begins. It continues for the life of your company's culture change. As you have seen, Implementation does not wait for the completion of such formalities as training. It begins the minute you spot a non-value-added step that compromises your performance. It proceeds parallel to the second, third, and fifth I's.

Reality Check _____

Subject Company: A computer tape-drive company
Source: John Swanson, TGI partner
Situation: Here, in Swanson's words, is a tale of a one-man Implementation campaign that climaxed after just the slightest touch of Inspiration.

SWANSON: I had a very bright and aggressive manufacturing engineer working for me named Gary. In addition to his technical skills, Gary's background included two tours of duty as an Army helicopter pilot in Vietnam. This experience developed in him a certain impatience with bureaucratic practices. His responsibilities now included the development of the manufacturing process for a new tape drive. One day, he needed to draw some parts from the stockroom in order to begin a pilot subassembly operation, and he encountered a business process barrier.

   After defining his parts needs, Gary went to the stockroom and requested service. Unfortunately, his visit occurred during the stockroom lunch period. The stockroom supervisor was at his desk eating his lunch and reading a newspaper, and he told Gary to return after lunch. Gary didn't want to be delayed; he wanted his parts *now*. The conversation continued for several minutes with each individual becoming more adamant. Finally, Gary lost patience and decided to use an alternative approach. He climbed the 10-foot-high chain link fence surrounding the stockroom and landed with both feet firmly planted in the middle of the stockroom supervisor's desk. Upon landing, he quickly obtained his parts from the shocked and now furious stockroom supervisor and went on his way. Approximately three minutes later, the stockroom supervisor and his boss were in my office demanding Gary's immediate dismissal for his "barrier removal" technique. (I subsequently complimented Gary on his dedication but suggested that he soften his approach somewhat.)

Conclusion: As much as I myself appreciate time warriors, I must reluctantly admit that Gary's surprise attack was a little *too* warlike. You can't assault a new system in so direct a manner, although we are all sorely tempted to try it from time to time.

Implementation begins early in any move to Total Cycle Time and remains in force for the duration of the move to entitlement.

Under conventional circumstances, the campaign of Implementation progresses systematically along the following lines:

- People with the appropriate know-how are pulled together into teams.
- The business process is modeled and examined.
- The steps of a business process are separated into value-added and non-value-added categories.
- Parts of the process that involve rework and delay or otherwise add no value are targeted and destroyed.
- The process is simplified.
- The process is measured by fewer but more relevant measurements than before.

During Implementation, many subject matter barriers will be exposed in the various subloops. On a more general basis, business process and cultural barriers or their symptoms will pop up (such as that Fairchild manager who was undermining the program, or Pressure Systems' "nonassertive management" culture that was at cross purposes with the company's goal). As you know, when these barriers are spotted and neutralized, ongoing feedback from your Cycles of Learning may expose others that were hidden beneath the first layer. Naturally, Implementation runs for the life of the culture change.

The gist of Implementation is simplification and shortening of business processes via detection and removal of non-value-added steps and barriers. Proper use of Cycles of Learning will expose old and new barriers.

Successful corporate Implementation produces some noteworthy side effects. One is psychological, a by-product of the fact that everything in the workplace is changing. Change can be very upsetting for workers whose security depends on a predictable, regular life. As new practices and measurements are implemented and old, comfortable ones go down the drain, the changeover can breed anxiety. When your old, familiar world comes crashing down, it is often hard to believe that it is all for the good and that you will ultimately be happier and more productive under a new Total Cycle Time culture. At this point, a leap of faith may be required — or a little arm-twisting by the managers higher up.

Hard to believe or not, the abandonment of comfortable but counterproductive steps must proceed. Although it may not seem so, you will grow comfortable again once the customary barriers are gone and the quality of your working environment improves. In fact, you will enjoy a level of psychological security you never felt under the old regime.

Reality Check _____

Subject Company: General Electric Ceramic, Inc., Chattanooga, Tennessee
Source: Paul Gallo, TGI partner
Situation: During a cycle time initiative at GECI, Paul Gallo encountered severe comfort curve problems. Morale was already low because of poor performance. The company's on-time deliveries had dropped to very low levels.

GALLO: GECI customers were continually calling the Customer Service and Production Control people to get the "latest" update on the already late deliveries of their orders. The

Production Control people would respond by going to the production line and resetting the production priorities each time the customer complained—the squeaky wheel syndrome. Often, by the end of a day, a production lot may have been rescheduled three or four times....LIFO (Last In, First Out) was often the reality. However, the condition that best fit production movement was FISH: First In, Still Here.

The morale at GECI was very poor, as most of the management and individual contributors were working 10 to 12 hours per day while making no noticeable progress. Customers continued to complain, profits continued to be negative, and most of their personal family lives were in turmoil.

It was readily apparent that some quick wins were needed if this team was to be inspired to move further into an improvement program. A one-time lot prioritization system was instituted for all product lots on the [production] floor.... The initial priority was based on the perceived customer requirements, starting with the lots nearest to the end of the line and working toward the front. All subsequent lots started in the line were given a consecutive priority code. Rules were set up that the lowest lot priority number (that is, the highest priority) was to be processed first at each production station with no exceptions. The priority could only be changed with the approval of the president. This process immediately forced the line to operate in a FIFO [First In, First Out] manner.

The Production Control people were now in total disarray because their primary job activity had gone away. As quoted by the Production Control manager: "We can no longer use our hands and feet to manage the line; we only have our minds."

Outcome: "The shock was at first overwhelming, and on several occasions the rules were clandestinely ignored. The perpetrator was always discovered and each time 'retrained.' The basic principle quickly became accepted when the priority process started to pay off in improved performance to schedule. Within 60 days—half the current cycle time—the customer complaint phone calls were reduced by 60 percent."

Morale issues aside, this story is a useful illustration of how Inspiration, Information, and Implementation proceed hand-in-hand.

Although it is the fourth of the Five I's, Implementation can begin the moment you spot an obvious barrier. Go for early, easy rewards. Pluck the low-hanging fruit!

Another noteworthy phenomenon is that the results of implementation often occur in step functions, not as a smoothly accelerating process, because barriers do not turn up obligingly at a regular pace. When, after the first layer of barriers is removed, cycle times stop falling and a company's performance levels off, you will need to remember that you are up against additional obstructions that were unseen until the surface barriers disappeared.

Reality Check _____

Subject Company: Texas Instruments
Situation: Texas Instruments was proud of having developed a highly automated dock-to-stock system to receive and process incoming orders. The system was a technological beauty, but necessary items were taking entirely too long to go from dock to stock, so they embarked on a formal effort to cut cycle times. They were taken through Inspiration. Lot sizes were cut and non-value-added steps eliminated. Multiple inspections were reduced, and as expected, cycle time dropped. Then the effort mysteriously stalled far from entitlement and wouldn't budge for almost three months.

Had expectations been set too high? No. The effort had struck a second-level barrier. It lay somewhere in the testing process through which large numbers of incoming components had to pass. The test area, it was discovered, was managed by a highly skilled triumvirate. One manager was an expert in manufacturing, another in quality, the other in engineering. Each had a long track record and a longstanding set of priorities and procedures he had developed independently of the other two.

Outcome: The company's laudable concern for expertise had spawned a department whose uncoordinated, repetitive procedures could hold up material at least three times longer than necessary. That significant three-into-one barrier had somehow escaped notice until, like a rock exposed by the falling tide, it blocked further passage. Simplifying the structure removed this barrier, allowing further barriers to be exposed and removed until entitlement was met.

Again, when progress stalls, don't take it as a sign that your entitlement expectations were too optimistic. It is instead a sign that there are more barriers to remove.

Implementation is a more complex process than the straightforward removal of barriers and reduction of cycle times. Do not expect Implementation to produce an uninterrupted climb to entitlement.

During Implementation, your company should begin to use measurements that are relevant to competitiveness. These will become permanent fixtures after entitlement. Meanwhile, the measurements will convert Inspiration to habit because you and your peers will be evaluated accordingly. Your company's progress during Implementation should be measured monthly by the following criteria:

- Competitiveness
- Cycle time (in all processes)
- First-pass yield
- Inventory and receivables reduction
- Customer satisfaction
- Sales and relative market share
- Profit
- People effectiveness

A word about the last measurement above. People effectiveness, discussed in Chapter 3, is the best measurement to determine how well a company's employees are being utilized because it takes into account the cost of employees, not the head count. As your company moves toward entitlement, it may pay to have more people who cost less or fewer people who cost more: three line workers, for example, instead of a manager. If doing so costs less overall, your company has improved its people effectiveness figure and enhanced overall employee motivation to continue the Total Cycle Time mindset.

More effective use of people is a predictable outcome of barrier removal, and one of the most demanding aspects of implementation is to prepare for that eventuality. Because shorter cycle times mean better people effectiveness, your company may experience a lag between increased productivity and the point at which business grows, through improved responsiveness, to meet that capacity. During this catch-up period there is likely to be a surplus of workers.

It would of course be a betrayal to repay improved employee productivity with layoffs, so your company should plan ahead for such techniques as cross-training, attrition policies, and possibly reduced hours per shift in order to keep the momentum of the new culture from slacking. Although such lags between increased capacity and increased business are by nature temporary, they should *never* be allowed to take the work force by surprise.

Reality Check _____

Subject Company: General Electric Ceramic, Inc.
Situation: At GECI, we were charged with improving performance in the company's make/market loop. By cutting back the input to the manufacturing operation and bringing down the work-in-process inventory, cycle time was reduced. Meanwhile, feedback loops were installed to utilize the resulting increase in Cycles of Learning, which dramatically raised first-pass yield. As rework and scrap diminished, so did the company's labor needs.

It was obvious that it would take a while for increased sales to overtake the new oversupply of labor, so by prior consultation with union leadership, one-third of the overall work force was laid off temporarily. When first faced with this problem, GECI's management preferred cutting back one complete shift instead of a balanced outback in each of the three shifts. Because cycle time is a function of the number of operating shifts, management would have actually lengthened the company's cycle time had it gotten its way.

Outcome: About three months later, everyone laid off at GECI was called back to a more secure, solid business.

As painful as layoffs are for a well-intentioned company, reducing the work force (especially in white-collar areas) can be very educational, even inspirational.

Reality Check _____

Source: Tom Oliveri, TGI partner
Situation: Here is Tom Oliveri's recollection of a California company's entitlement struggle.

OLIVERI: The market for one of the company's core product lines was disappearing rapidly, and it became clear that a major downsizing of the company would lead to significant layoffs....To the company's credit, a number of strategic actions had been taken without which the loss of this core business might have been fatal. The company went forward with a series of layoffs.

Twelve percent of the company's jobs were eliminated, generating great concern on the part of management.

OLIVERI: When the smoke cleared from the layoffs, a number of interesting phenomena were observed. First of all, people looked around and discovered that all the key players in the cycle time reduction program were still there. In fact, two of them were promoted to the vice-presidential level. This was not lost on other employees. Levels of interest and participation in the cycle time reduction program actually

seemed to go up rather than down following the layoffs.
Although the layoffs had a predictably negative impact on
overall morale, performance seemed less affected and
morale rebounded more quickly among the people involved
in the cycle time reduction program.

Conclusion: Tom Oliveri's team purposely played no part in
deciding *who* should be laid off, and participation in the cycle
time reduction program was not considered a criterion for
who would stay. Nonetheless, an interesting pattern emerged.

OLIVERI: The same kind of smart, aggressive, hard-working
   managers who jumped at the chance to remove the barriers
   frustrating them turned out to be the same kind of
   employees that a company wants to keep around during a
   downsizing. [Cycle-time-reduction] provided a rallying point
   for these employees during the bad times the company was
   passing through.
      Second, it is not necessary to guarantee jobs in order to
   entice employees to participate in a program to reduce cycle
   time and improve performance. In fact, such a guarantee
   could prove counterproductive if it attracts poor performers
   who are motivated by fear for their jobs instead of strong
   performers who really want to make things work better.
   Finally, it should be clear that a company going through [a]
   changing market environment must improve its processes if
   it expects to survive and be competitive.

As with weight loss programs, when momentum slackens,
confusion and discouragement may set in. At such times, one
need only remember that the laws of nature apply to everyone and that sticking to the program will sooner or later yield
the desired results.

The Fifth I: Internalization

Most people who manage to shed weight fail to keep it off for
any length of time. To avoid becoming part of that statistic,

when you get the results anticipated, you must make sure to keep them. That requires cultivating a new attitude toward eating, which amounts to a culture change in a business.

Easier said than done, I'll admit, because regressions happen. The force of bad habits can be enormous. As I said above, I still have to bite my tongue when that dessert cart goes by. I know I can do it, though, because the rewards of staying trim outweigh my previous romance with dining. It's the internalization of a new mindset.

Internalization is the last of Total Cycle Time's Five I's. Internalization is a process of behavior modification by which you discard your unwholesome work habits and actually commit yourself to new ones. Each of the Five I's is essential to lasting competitive performance, but somehow Internalization is often neglected in the afterglow of reaching entitlement—a grave mistake. Four out of five I's is not good enough.

Reaching entitlement does not complete the conversion to Total Cycle Time. Once the goal is reached, managers often lose interest or discontinue those critical new measurements or forget to follow through with the idea that the company is on a *continuous* improvement course. There is also frequently a change of management (often through promotion) after reaching entitlement, which brings unaccultured leaders aboard. Internalization is your and your company's insurance against backsliding to baseline.

Throughout this book, as with every company's move to Total Cycle Time, I advocate the adoption of a new mindset. That is part of Internalization. But the fifth I is more than simply a change of attitude. It is also a *process* by which your company preserves TCT culture for the future. Internalization includes these safeguards:

- A hierarchical set of measurements, recognition, and rewards that are consistent with the new culture and are installed as early in the Five I's process as practical.

- A strategy to exploit your company's superior response capability.

- A periodic reexamination of your potential for performance improvement.

- A continuous program of improving competitiveness through technology, training, tools, and the database provided by Cycles of Learning.

Because these steps are so often overlooked, each one merits a brief discussion.

A Hierarchical Set of Measurements

A new, hierarchical set of measurements consistent with your company's new culture is the most significant factor in maintaining long-range competitiveness. At entitlement, your company will have adopted measurements and controls that fit the new culture while discarding those that don't. Which ones don't?

Those that do not drive the Three R's

Those that focus on deliverables, functions, or subject matter

Those that are manipulable (such as performance to internally created schedules, cost of quality, and functional rating data)

Those that track non-value-added activity

Those that are self-serving

The extent to which people can manipulate the wrong criteria is sometimes astonishing, as the following example shows. This classic case turned up at a company plant in the late 1980s; management was kidding itself about on-time delivery. Records showed deliveries to be almost 99 percent on schedule, but here was the catch: Because the plant suffered from poor designs, limited testing capacity, and low yields, the VP and director of planning adopted a policy to measure performance to the latest *"current schedule"* date instead of the customer's requested date or the originally scheduled ship date. "Current schedule" could be changed by the plan-

ning group at any time. No wonder the company could claim
that its performance to schedule was almost perfect.

So sacred was the principle of keeping to schedule that
even product finished by a customer's request date would be
held longer if the in-house programming had scheduled delivery for a later date! In other words, management was willing to be delinquent in the customer's eyes so long as performance fitted its oft-revised internal schedule. The moral
here: Never underestimate the power of cultural myopia or
the allure of improper measurements.

Reality Check

Subject Company: Coleman Outdoor Products
Source: Bonnie Sloan, TGI partner
Situation: Coleman, a venerable producer of camping stoves
and equipment, had its employees on an "incentive" pay
system based on the number of piece parts produced. That
measurement had been in place for close to a century and was
a cultural paradigm at Coleman. But it was an improper
measurement. As Bonnie Sloan saw it, "In the interest of
keeping parts flowing so operators could make their 'rate,'
parts were being overbuilt, and rework was created
knowingly."
Outcome: Coleman, however, was determined to adopt the
entitlement mindset. Accordingly, "the pay (measurement)
system was changed, and significant gains in first-pass yield
and inventory reduction were made. Even 90-year cultures can
be changed when a company is committed to a Total Cycle
Time program."

Which measurements *do* fit the new culture? The following,
most of which you came to know during Implementation:

Cycle times

First-pass yield

Cycles of Learning

People effectiveness

Percentage of on-time delivery

Inventory levels (they should be minimal)

Total product cost

Return on cash tied up

Notice that the new measurements must be hierarchical. That means they must be consistent from top to bottom in your company. Measurements at your level should thus have like counterparts above and below. Those that don't should be discarded.

Hierarchical measurements are clear. They are simple. They are driven by your company's responsiveness to customers, and they can be tracked from the top. They are not *manipulable.*

When hierarchical measurements become the basis for individual evaluation, everyone in your company, even cultural holdouts, will be forced to come permanently to terms with the new culture and operate on a common basis.

Reality Check _____

Subject Company: A major pharmaceutical company
Source: Richard Joyce, TGI Sr. partner
Situation: Cycle time of course tops the list of proper measurements. The power of that measurement comes across in the following story:

JOYCE: The group controller of the company noticed the improved financial performance at the division and decided to attend our next cycle time review. During the meeting, he said he was pleased with many financial results but surprised that the review was so simple and focused on cycle time. Asked how many key measurements he dealt with, he responded that "corporate" required nearly two dozen, "group" two dozen more, and that each of the divisions added their own — maybe 80 total. I explained that the reason cycle time focus works so well is that it is an independent variable in nearly all key business measurements, and I used schedule, cost, quality, and inventory as examples. [*An independent variable is a factor that can be changed independently of others but, when changed, exerts an impact on the others.*]

When the meeting ended, we went to lunch. The controller sought me out there and said that during the meeting, he reviewed all of the corporate and group measurements in his mind and found that over 90 percent had cycle time as an independent variable. Most major ones that didn't were human resources: turnover, etc. Of course, I countered that cycle time reduction...increased job satisfaction and reduced turnover.

A Strategy to Exploit Superior Response

A strategy to exploit superior response should be considered *before* your company reaches entitlement. This is a matter of developing a plan to exploit the market advantages that will come your way when you can outmaneuver your competition.

In almost every case, entitlement companies find that there are significant ways to leverage their superior responsiveness. In some instances, there are opportunities to change forever the standard of an entire industry. Again, Federal Express is an example. Fed Ex rewrote the standard for mail delivery, making it an overnight activity. And with the increasing shift toward custom as opposed to standardized products, responsive companies have the winning hand. In addition, they can offer the customer the prerogative of changing his or her mind, a feature that has commercial possibilities.

The playing field at entitlement is much different — and more promising — than at baseline. Your company must plan accordingly.

Periodic Reexaminations of Improvement Potential

A periodic reexamination is much like an individual's once-a-year physical checkup. Actually, a year is too long between personal competitiveness checkups. If you've thus far followed the advice given here, you check your cycle time and first-pass yield *daily*. You should also review your performance at least quarterly with your boss.

Old habits die hard. With time, some once-entrenched measurements and controls may raise their ugly heads again because they were not totally eradicated from the corporate mindset. That is why a competitive company needs an annual reexamination, during which it compares its current performance to its entitlement figures to make certain no significant barriers have appeared or reappeared. A formal annual checkup also allows your company to test whether its post-entitlement strategic thrust is proceeding to plan and whether everyone is getting the most from Cycles of Learning.

Daily review of cycle time and first-pass yield keeps you on your toes. Quarterly review with your boss keeps you both on the same cultural wave length. Annual reexaminations keeps a competitive company from becoming complacent and prevents old process and cultural viruses from flaring up.

A Continuous Program of Improved Competitiveness

A continuous program of improved competitiveness applies Cycles of Learning, new methods of barrier identification and removal, and whatever general breakthroughs occur throughout an industry, with the goal of steepening the rate of the improvement curve achieved at entitlement.

Entitlement is not a static condition. New developments, learning, and the repeated dividends of feedback continually increase the potential for competitive performance.

During the Internalization phase, previously unforeseen gaps in the Five I's are apt to surface — barriers that must be eliminated to ensure the endurance of the new culture.

Reality Check

Subject Company: Wacker Chemietronic, Burghausen, Germany
Source: Peter Idell, TGI partner
Situation: In 1988–1990, Wacker undertook their cycle time reduction initiative. The project began in a single Wacker facility and grew from there, but it did not embrace every element of the company.

IDELL: Wacker had made major progress in the fifteen-month program but had not [everywhere] reached entitlement, was continually backsliding, and had not truly institutionalized the Total Cycle Time mindset.

Results would have been much better had the entire operation been involved. Instead, Peter recalls, "Some products were manufactured using the people and equipment allocated from the Standard Line, which was not involved in the Total Cycle Time program.
Meanwhile, Internalization of the achieved results revealed some surprises.

IDELL: The first surprise was that the general manager of the Advanced and Standard Lines had started in his position *after* the Total Cycle Time program had been initiated and had never received proper training. It also soon became clear that although the organization had plans and goals for the coming year, they were not tied together into a unified hierarchical set.

There were other reasons that Wacker had not reached its entitlement. For example, parts of the company that had not been included in our project had tried to cut cycle times on their own, with mixed results. Elsewhere, well-intentioned managers, bumping against unperceived barriers, mistook those obstructions for the upper limit of their performance and declared themselves at entitlement. Meanwhile, pockets of excess inventory continued to pile up.

Conclusion: The long and short of it was that at Wacker, Internalization was incomplete, largely because some corporate sectors had not been exposed to the new culture in force. The company had learned four key lessons.

IDELL: The caveat against "less than total" programs is real, the need for Inspiration of *all* the key players is real, the need for top-down commitment and appropriate measures is imperative, and the opportunity for improvements at Wacker is better than it has ever been.

Internalization is the final phase of the Five I's. Although easily overlooked or underestimated, Internalization is absolutely essential if your company intends to remain competitive.

Living successfully with a new corporate culture is a matter of attitude modification — a new mindset — and behavior modification. Accepting short-cycle-time thinking as second nature constitutes the former, imposition of formal measurements and controls constitutes the latter. Both are indispensable.

How Long Will It Take?

The time required to move from baseline to entitlement is a function of your company's size, the degree of its decentralization, and the depth of its cultural barriers. However, you may find the scale in the table on page 149 helpful.

Even cycle time specialists must constantly work to reduce cycle times. In our case, that is the time we need to successfully deliver *institutionalized* results to customers.

Company size (annual sales)	Years to reach entitlement
$ 10 million	1.0
100 million	1.5
500 million	2.2
1 billion	3.0
3 billion	4.3

When Are We Through?

Never. Total Cycle Time is not a program or a phase your company is going through. It is a new corporate culture. And if you keep your mind on retaining and advancing it, you can grow old together. This is a journey with a beginning but no end.

When your company has completed the Five I's, it is by definition a winner—formidably competitive. Like someone who has mastered weight loss and behavior modification, your company will be lean and confident, able to move quickly to secure and improve its sector of the market. If your company is that way, you will be too.

7

Individual Tactics to Win the Time War

Even the Experts Have Room to Improve

Just before undertaking this chapter, I witnessed a sterling example of individual self-empowerment, of which I was the major beneficiary. Here is the story.

Reality Check: Self-Empowerment _____

Subject: Angie McMahon, TGI support partner

Situation: I had an assessment to do at a petrochemical company in Houston, but my assistant, Debbie Barber, was unable to accompany me, so I drafted Angie McMahon, my second assistant, for the trip.

My assessments include several 45-minute interviews with key insiders. Over the years, after each interview, I have developed the habit of dictating 10 minutes' worth of notes on each encounter to an assistant typing on a laptop computer. Later, back at the office, those notes have been edited and the resulting material made into an orientation package for the appointed program manager. That was the accepted method until the day of the petrochemical interviews.

That morning in Houston, before I could head for the first subject's office, he intercepted me in a conference room where Angie and I were working at opposite ends of a conference table. Rather than waste time, I conducted the interview right there. As the two of us talked, I became aware of the unobtrusive clacking of Angie's laptop keyboard, but neither I nor my subject paid it any mind. After the interview, however, Angie called me to her workplace and asked, "What do you think of this?" I was amazed to find that she had been listening and had directly typed the entire interview, editing as she went along to fit the intended report's final format. Angie had slashed cycle time, improved the content, and raised the quality of the report in one fell swoop. As she put it, typing up a real-time version of each interview was "the same as if the program manager had sat in on your initial assessment of the situation." We did the rest of the day's interviews the same way, with Angie and her laptop sitting in on each interview.

Conclusion: By the time we had finished, I knew this was a breakthrough. Gone was the need to dictate from scribbled notes. Gone was the need for an assistant to edit and collate that work. Gone was the wait for that process to unfold. On her own initiative, Angie had pinpointed a process barrier and eliminated it, just like that. Such breakthroughs can become frequent occurrences in any company whose employees feel they are empowered to exploit their initiative.

The New Culture of Empowerment

As companies around the world battle for competitiveness, a heartening new weapon is finding its way into many corporate cultures: empowerment. Generally speaking, *empowerment* denotes the phenomenon in which authority to take decisive action is delegated from the top downward through the managerial chain of command. But time and again, while watching a company fight its way from baseline to entitlement, I have seen individual employees exercise power out of all proportion to their place within the formal structure. This change often occurs within an official setup such as a cross-functional team. But it also proceeds informally as people throughout an organization realize that removing non-value-added steps and barriers while raising first-pass yield is everybody's business. As that attitude takes hold, individual time warriors like Angie gain additional firepower with which to secure their objectives.

The Components of Empowerment

Empowerment should become an integral part of any organization that is competitive or is moving in that direction. It should have the trust, understanding, and support of employees, managers, customers, and owners. In such environments, individuals are encouraged to:

- Accept the right, risk, *and* responsibility to fail a little in return for increasing their Cycles of Learning.

- Champion a cause, confront an issue, and remove a barrier without unreasonable fear of reprisal.

- Continuously expand their capacity *and* power to cause change up, down, and across the organization, based on their grasp of issues and track record.

Empowerment packs a wallop for any company's future. For one thing, it gives individuals the authority and confidence to strike a decisive blow for the greater good, attacking barriers above and beyond the conventional limits of employee power. By treating barrier removal as an objective issue which does not jeopardize the formal chain of command, companies liberate a potent, untapped store of employee energy. Thus, no matter where they are in their company's pecking order, time warriors who approach problems with the objective criteria, terminology, and mindset of Total Cycle Time can make a meaningful, positive difference.

Eliminating the Fear of Failure and Risk

When discussing the issue of empowerment, many employees in the lower organizational levels say that it is valid in principle but risky in practice. But empowerment and fear of failure cannot coexist in a truly competitive organization. Apprehensions most often arise when employees fear they cannot make a process work as required or that they cannot successfully implement changes that will make a positive difference. Both of those fears are carryovers from a long-cycle-time environment.

Long-cycle-time processes are inherently unpredictable. People who work under such conditions often get blamed for their unpredictability even though they are clearly its victims. Furthermore, with long cycle times, Cycles of Learning are so few that remedial steps, though selected in good conscience, often turn out to be substitute processes or patch-up solutions that actually worsen performance in the long run.

Short-cycle-time processes reduce or eliminate fear of failure. In addition, there is general understanding that a few failures here and there are a by-product of rapid Cycles of Learning; therefore, such occurrences carry no stigma. In other words, fear of failure does not obstruct empowerment or discourage initiative.

Empowerment and Opportunity

Empowerment is especially fitted to business in the United States because it requires every employee to get involved in barrier identification ("Does this step add value?") and removal ("It doesn't, so I won't do it"). That sort of mindset harmonizes with traditional U.S. individualism.

Empowerment is not likely to take root everywhere among the competition, however. In Asian companies especially, nonmanagerial employees will find it almost impossible to say no. Their national and corporate cultures are not built for that. In the United States, the winners will be those companies and individuals that accept empowerment as a dynamic tool for entitlement. Which brings the story back to you.

In Chapter 6, you saw the mechanics of Total Cycle Time expressed in terms of their companywide application. The purpose of this chapter is to discuss the Five I's at a personal level to help you merge your own objectives with the process. If your company has decided to adopt Total Cycle Time, these tips will add to the momentum and sharpen your participation. If you are still on your own, they will get you started on a professional self-improvement program. (They should also get you started on a self-empowerment program!)

You and the Five I's

The Five I's are easy to appreciate in terms of corporate competitiveness. Assuming you accept the principles involved, you still may be unsure of how to apply them personally. You are probably also wondering how far someone in the trenches can go individually. That is quite understandable. For these reasons, the approach to this next section will be through a list of the questions most commonly asked by individuals like yourself. Here they are, "I by I."

Getting Inspired

What gets people like me inspired?

Two things. The first is credibility. You must believe that Total Cycle Time is a pragmatic, hands-on approach to improving performance which will multiply your personal job satisfaction and is therefore worth fighting for. This book, for example, is intended to serve that objective.

A second type of Inspiration occurs when individuals like yourself actually see the first results of barrier removal. You make those results, and through Cycles of Learning, you accelerate their pace.

How do I stay inspired?

There are three techniques for when you feel overwhelmed by inertia around you:

- Remind yourself regularly of the key points of short-cycle-time thinking — Cycles of Learning, barrier removal, reduction of actions in process, and removal of non-value-added steps.
- Maintain your own momentum in removing barriers.
- Rally others to the cause and leverage the benefits of collective Cycles of Learning. Try staying focused on what there is to gain. After all, what's to lose?

You have to live with the Total Cycle Time mindset until it's second nature. Meanwhile, don't hesitate to strike out at targets you have identified in the business process. As soon as you have streamlined your own subject matter area, help yourself to some low-hanging fruit by attacking a process step that adds no value to your work.

When you have identified such process barriers, you have an opportunity to involve your peers and boss in the new mindset. Remember, there is strength in numbers, and a squad of time warriors packs a lot more firepower than you can muster as a single sharpshooter. All of you should discuss where and how to say no and stick to your guns.

How do I inspire my peers?

When you start getting results in your personal area, you are certain to arouse curiosity among your coworkers. That's important, because the best way to inspire peers is by example. By all means share your new mindset with others. (Feel free to alert them to this book, if it has helped you.) Like you, your colleagues need to see that barrier removal is everybody's business and that the biggest enemies to competitiveness lie within the company's business processes and culture.

When you break your campaign out among your peers, you might try a method used to jump-start cross-functional teams. Before you meet, have each potential time warrior prepare a personal list of his or her actions in process to share with the group. (An overhead projector or chalk board will help if there are more than two of you.) Everyone in the group is then given the chance to question and critique every action on every list. Peers have a way of asking embarrassing questions about a process that you or someone else may take for granted (or even hold sacred). In any case, there are always the old reliables:

> Does it drive one or more of the three R's? No? Then it ought to go.

> Does it add value to the company? Yes? How much value?

Believe me, the jump-start technique really works as a group inspirational tool at all levels.

How can I carry the message upstairs?

This question need not trouble you if your company understands that cycle time drives effective performance. But even if no one but you has discovered Total Cycle Time, you can bet that your superiors are consciously searching for ways to get competitive. In fact, you can even bet that they're *preoccupied* with that issue. Typical CEOs spend up to half their time planning how to differentiate the company from the competition. Such preoccupation diminishes proportionately in middle and lower levels of management, but, to some extent, performance is on everybody's mind.

If your company is operating without benefit of a formal strategy for the time war, your task is to share your personal entitlement figures with your boss, demonstrating some of the gains you will have made through barrier removal. Timing, however, is important. If possible, talk to the boss only after you've made headway and swapped ideas with your peers.

Don't flinch; Total Cycle Time works. Accordingly, you and your peers have a good chance of pushing the ethic up the ladder. If you're convinced you don't have enough rank to go face-to-face with your superior without preparation, there is an alternative. After you and your peers have a session or two under your belts, invite your boss to the next one. In our own Implementation seminars, we break managers into just such a group—several peers and their immediate superior—and assign each team the task of determining the impact of short cycle times on their sector of the corporation. The presence of the boss eliminates a lot of peer-group hot air and ensures instant, usually positive feedback. Everybody quickly understands that barrier removal is everybody's business.

Speaking of everybody's business, there is also much to be gained in having your peers and superiors adopt the Total Cycle Time terminology used here—baseline, entitlement, Cycles of Learning, substitute processes, first-pass yield, actions in process, non-value-added, and so forth—as soon as possible. Speaking a common language of competitiveness is one of the most important steps in actually achieving competitiveness. Be sure to express yourself accordingly at any and every opportunity. Those terms force people to think in different, more competitive ways and thereby accelerate acceptance of the new mindset. As soon as possible, you should share your personal flow diagram with your peers and boss so that they can carry out that process too. They, like you, will then come to realize that their chief enemies are internal barriers, not external forces.

Reality Check

Subject Process: Customer Service
Source: Bill Wield, TGI partner
Situation: Here is a case in which the kind of familiarization just described saved the job of a customer service supervisor at a company in Ireland. The service center's inability to deal promptly with customer returns was causing a major uproar among top managers. It was company policy to rebuild all returned merchandise virtually by hand, a time-consuming and laborious process, and because the center had no way of anticipating the volume of returns, it could not pace itself properly. Cycle times lengthened unacceptably to 50 days, customers got angrier, and the center's beleaguered supervisor knew his days were numbered.

A management workshop was held in which everyone had to map out the process flow for items returned to the company by customers.

Outcome

WIELD: The result was the startling realization of what the supervisor had to deal with. Before that, management did not realize the details of the process and its associated disconnects. Management made cycle time a key measurement. Additional barriers were identified, prioritized, and removed. The cycle time was reduced to 25 days. The supervisor kept his job. Management is now using the mapping process to ensure that supervisors and employees understand the causes of job performance.

A pointer: When you discuss barriers with your boss, make certain that he or she has either mapped the process in a fashion similar to your own or has shared the results of your own efforts.

Doing Your Own Identification

What loop am I a part of?

Your own sphere of activity is of course part of a wider sphere that connects with a major loop, be it design/ development or make/market. Remember those barrier circles discussed in Chapter 5? If you are an order entry clerk, for example, your daily responsibility is only two circles away from the operational VP's. Or if you provide pricing information to field sales people, you are a key part of the marketing process, and your improved performance will have a powerful positive effect on the overall loop.

Now, barrier circles being what they are, an improvement in performance within your subloop or subprocess will create a ripple effect that reaches the outer edge of the business. That is why creative empowerment is so important a concept.

Where should I start? Where should I stop?

You start by taking a piece of paper, listing your own actions in process, diagramming your own business process, and then computing your personal baseline and entitlement as described in Chapter 4. Your diagram will provide clues to the general process outside your immediate area by fixing your input and output points in the process. (Input and output points are the ones at which you receive a request for action and complete the request, respectively.) That should come in handy when you talk to others.

Can I reliably set my own entitlement?

The method of computing entitlement described in Chapter 4 is accurate, but it must be done with care. Furthermore, you should use each of the computation methods to confirm the accuracy of your work:

- Quantifying the effect of the process barriers confronting you

- Analyzing your historical best and worst performance figures

- Calculating your theoretical cycle time

The need for care is stressed because objectivity often suffers during Identification. There is a powerful urge to give yourself the benefit of the doubt or to simply overlook barriers that are staring you in the face. If, after using all three techniques to compute your entitlement, your figures don't make sense, you had better reexamine the process, for you have overlooked some key barriers.

Getting Your Own Information

Where can I find more how-to information?

Currently, getting information on time-based management is admittedly tough. If you read the *Wall Street Journal* or various business magazines, you are probably already aware that time-based management is a very lively subject. Yet if you browse in the business section of your local bookstore, you will find that the pickings are mighty slim. The problem is that very few writers actually understand the practical realities of the subject. What has been written is usually long on theory and wishful thinking but short on workable, proven directions on getting the job done.

If your company has not consciously embraced Total Cycle Time, it would behoove you to talk to someone whose company has. That someone need not be in your line of work, because the competitiveness crisis is general, and most barriers, as you now know, are generic. By the same token, it is not important that he or she work at your approximate level. What *is* important is that when you do compare notes, you use an objective lingo and set of concepts such as those comprised by Total Cycle Time.

The importance of learning to spot the barriers that obstruct the business process outside your immediate subject matter domain cannot be overstressed. These barriers are the biggest enemies of competitiveness. And to defeat them, a time warrior may have to snatch a little self-empowerment.

Initiating Personal Implementation

How do I spot the low-hanging fruit?

Low-hanging fruit is not simply a phrase for barriers that are immediately apparent and easily toppled. The term designates those barriers whose removal produces a quick and sizable surge in personal or company performance.

To identify low-hanging fruit, rank-order the barriers you've exposed before taking action. If, for example, you've found three non-value-added steps which tie up 4, 5, and 12 percent of your effort, respectively, by all means go after the 12 percenter without delay. You can thus make a big splash, which should attract peer attention and improve your morale. A few early victories can keep Inspiration at a peak.

A surprising number of individuals and companies labor under branches so heavy with low-hanging fruit that removal would make a profound difference.

Reality Check _____

Subject Process: Design and Construction of steam
generation plants

Situation: Analysis of a company that designed and built
steam generation plants revealed a clear need to cut its
two-year cycle times in half, for if that were possible, all sorts
of business opportunities would open up. We systematically
sought out ways to hasten these objectives. We looked for, and
found, some low-hanging fruit.

To begin with, it was possible to shorten the client's
engineering process by creating parallel paths, reordering the
process and eliminating a few generic design barriers. But it
was also possible to cut radically the time needed for plant
construction.

One of the most important components of steam plants is
pipe, the procurement of which takes many months. Because
pipe represents a significant part of a plant's construction cost,
company engineers worked long and hard to optimize this
cost. When it came to minimizing pipe requirements, their
plant designs were precise to a fault. And they took forever.

Waiting for precise designs minimized the cost of pipe, and,
indeed, the company seldom bought a dime's worth more than
it needed. But because pipe could not be ordered until the
design was finished, the process greatly lengthened delivery
cycle time. Meanwhile, people and equipment were tied up,
making the cost of that delay greater than the saving on pipe.
By optimizing its pipe costs, the company was not serving its
customers' best interests and was losing major opportunities.
Early completion of a plant could save customers as much as
$200,000 a day, so shaving half a year off the construction
time would bring new customers flocking.

Conclusion: There was the low-hanging fruit. (If it had
hung any lower, the pipe-cost-obsessed engineers would have
had to walk around it!) In the time it took to change the order
of engineering and abandon the fixation on pipe costs, our
client could dramatically cut its delivery times and be in the
running for time-based contracts.

On the second day of a recent executive seminar, a participant confided that since his arrival, he had received 35 voice
mail calls, only 2 of which had any value-added content. In

his office environment, calls had seemed a legitimate part of his routine. But once he was far enough away to reconsider his daily grind and apply the value-added test, their true nature became clear. That executive's competitiveness is worth quite a bit per second to his company. Devising a process to screen himself from non-value-added intrusion will require some administrative thinking, but once it is in place, he will save an enormous chunk of time and money each day. And this is a kind of low-hanging fruit that applies to vast numbers of people in the business world.

How do I spot the more subtle generic barriers?

Or rather, "How difficult is it to spot them?" As you probably noticed when you did your flow chart, some generic process barriers, such as the voice mail example just cited, are so annoying that they stick out like sore thumbs (or low-hanging fruit). But not all are so obvious. If you use Chapter 5's generic list as a guide, you should be able to expose quite a few inconspicuous barriers as well.

As your search progresses, you may find that substitute processes are your major headache. In fact, I've seen cases where individuals discovered that their entire jobs revolved around the care and feeding of indefensible substitute processes. In one instance, a manager at a *Fortune* 500 company supervised 54 people who did nothing but unscramble screwups in the company's order entry process. Imagine, more than four dozen employees dedicated to untangling the mistakes of other employees! As luck would have it, this manager embraced Total Cycle Time heart and soul. Concluding that his department was a living substitute process, he worked with the order entry business process to eliminate errors and thus raise first-pass yield. Eventually, his organization was reduced to four.

Most people, quite understandably, would be reluctant to commit career hara-kari by announcing their redundancy. Nonetheless, such reluctance is part of an old mindset. Under the new, if you have discovered a barrier or substitute process, there is no reasonable alternative to striving for its removal. Otherwise, you are collaborating knowingly in a no-win, no-security situation in which your company's competitive position worsens. In case you see such handwriting on the wall, I hasten to add that by exposing substitute processes at the risk of their jobs, quite a few alert people have freed themselves for better uses by their grateful companies.

How do I use Cycles of Learning at the personal level?

As soon as you have established your baseline and entitlement and have adopted the measurements discussed below, it is time to add Cycles of Learning to your personal barrier demolition kit. You begin by determining how many cycles you undergo in a year. Compute the number by dividing the number of work days per year by your cycle time. If you work 240 days annually and your cycle time is two days, you have 120 opportunities to learn in a single year.

Remember: Cycles of Learning are among the most potent weapons available for corporate and individual performance improvement. But opportunities don't become Cycles of Learning unless you receive and analyze their feedback and keep the corrective actions in process within the feedback loop low. Do this as often as possible. Once a week at the very least, you must look at your performance measurements and ask yourself how they could be improved:

"My first-pass yield is 92 percent.

What is causing 8 percent scrap or rework?

How can I reduce the percentage?"

If you are working within a resource-hungry, long-cycle-time culture, it's a good bet that almost nobody is looking at performance your way. That makes your work and your results especially important.

How do I get empowered?

Theoretically, empowerment is handed down from above. But in a competitive culture, unofficial empowerment becomes a way of life. Time warriors should therefore get accustomed to exceeding their structured responsibilities whenever a problem raises its head. And as GE learned from the incident described in Chapter 5, self-empowerment can teach management some important lessons.

But not many companies are truly competitive. Therefore, it is prudent to remember that in an uncompetitive company, barrier removal is about the *only* area where self-empowerment is *not* risky.

Self-Initiated Cross-Functional Teams

Creating cross-functional teams is one means to empower skilled people who may lack managerial clout. The effectiveness of such teams increases as the new mindset takes hold in a company. Cross-functional teams have two major assets: They are empowered by management to identify and remove barriers and thus have official blessing, and they bring together people from all sides of a problem to attack it with the big picture in mind.

But cross-functional teams do not have to be mandated by management. What if, after identifying a process barrier, you approach whoever is on the other side of that barrier, compare notes, and determine a plan of attack? You and your counterpart have just established an effective, two-person, cross-functional team without having to wait for official blessing. A perfect example appeared in Chapter 5, when Stu Frank took Mary Malloy to lunch to iron out his paperwork problem.

Brainstorming to Flush Out Barriers

When you meet with peers or members of a cross-functional team, you should try a formal brainstorming technique. Here's how: Everyone in the group defines why he or she thinks a process doesn't work better. Each participant makes suggestions, which are noted and recorded without comment until all ideas are exhausted. At that point you've got a comprehensive list of barriers. Brainstorming is a quick way to get possible barriers onto the table while warming participants to the issues. It furthermore gives everyone a taste of potential empowerment.

Should I wait for my company to launch a cycle time reduction program or take action on my own?

You know the answer to this one. If nobody upstairs is listening, it's up to you — at least for a while. By making such a personal start, you will be instituting a guerrilla action in the time war. There are three points to remember about guerrilla warfare:

---

1. *Working from within, guerrillas are characteristically effective at exposing the internal weakness of a system.*

2. *Guerrilla efforts are almost always noted by the established power structure.*

3. *In the long run, however, guerrilla warfare is not sufficient to defeat and reform an entrenched establishment.*

Although it is true that a company's culture can be permanently altered only from the top down, that is no excuse for not simplifying your own sector of the business process and creating a *pocket of excellence.* If your subloop improves its responsiveness, accelerates its results, and makes better use of resources — the essence of the Three R's — it will make a financial difference and someone higher up will take note.

Upper management often seems insulated from the front lines by a concrete ceiling (given time war conditions, it's more like a concrete bunker), but there are numerous documented cases, such as an employee's refusal to carry out a non-value-added assignment, in which top brass have been profoundly influenced by results from below.

If you really want to get managers' attention, show them numbers. Here's an old but true personal anecdote to illustrate. When I converted TI's Custom Digital operations to short cycle time, it was an entirely self-propelled effort. Total Cycle Time was just in its infancy. And even though no issue was made of the matter (as I'm now urging you to do), the results were too conspicuous to escape top management's notice. Accordingly, I was surprised one day to receive a visit from TI's Semiconductor Group VP, J. Fred Bucy, who appeared at my office door for a personal look around. What was going on here, he wondered, that the rest of his managers were not doing? He soon got the picture and shortly thereafter had me make a presentation at the company's annual planning meeting. He followed my report with his own pointed instructions to the effect that the other managers should run their businesses like mine. It warmed my heart, to say the least.

Results, of course, always speak louder than rationale. But one way or another, your boss and your boss's boss have got to take the time warrior message to heart, because senior management's participation is purely and simply a prerequisite for survival. People in the lower ranks, however skilled and motivated, cannot overcome companywide cultural inertia by setting an inspiring example. Therefore, if your company still works according to a baseline mindset, and if you intend to find job satisfaction without moving, empowering yourself is inescapable.

In other words, you have a mission. Begin with your own workplace, confer with your peers, and when you've seen some results, talk to your boss. It just could be the first crack in that concrete ceiling.

How risky is self-empowerment and implementation?

Could you get yourself fired? It's possible, especially in companies whose managers resist as a matter of principle any original, unsolicited improvements. Those companies are scarcer than they used to be, of course. By now, most have either failed or changed culture in the nick of time. There are, however, some sectors where the new mindset has scarcely penetrated—banks and insurance companies, for example. If you are stuck in a noncompetitive firm where the concrete ceiling is truly uncrackable, have the guts to get out. It's only a matter of time. Meanwhile, you've acquired the skills to know a competitive company when you see one.

Reality Check _____

Subject Company: The Allstate Research and Planning Center, Menlo Park, California
Source: Steve Patent, TGI partner
Situation: Steve Patent is an example of this last premise. In 1982, he was employed at Allstate's research and planning center in Menlo Park, California.

PATENT: While working on a study of our Michigan auto policy holders, I called our Michigan headquarters to help answer a question about an anomaly in our data concerning claim amounts. The next day, my manager informed me that any question for field offices must be routed through the VP of underwriting in the Illinois home office.

Steve could see the consequence of such a process.

PATENT: Long cycle times for simple questions. Many questions never got asked, and I felt like a child who needed to ask Daddy's permission for everything. I decided to leave the company a few months later. Company cultures that assume that all wisdom comes from the top become self-fulfilling prophecies. People in lower ranks with any intelligence don't stick around.

For the most part, companies do in fact take notice of individuals who improve performance, rewarding and promoting them accordingly. It simply makes sense for management to give more command to time warriors. Managers also know that when promoted, the positive impact of those individuals will increase geometrically.

Personalizing the Fifth I: Internalization

How can I measure myself against the Three R's?

Developing a proper set of personal measurements is crucial to maintaining your individual performance improvement. Your first step in achieving this is to determine how you are measured at present. Do you know? Like so many others, you may find on reflection that you can't come up with a precise answer. That should tell you something. You will probably find that you are measured by subjective criteria that are hard to quantify. You are also likely to discover that the two most critical measurements of an individual, cycle time and first-pass yield, are missing altogether.

Once you have listed the items on which you are measured, test each one:

- Does it drive you toward improving the competitiveness of your company?
- Does it conflict with any of the Three R's?

If a measurement does not stimulate you to improve responsiveness to the customer, accelerate results, or minimize resources required, it is not a relevant measurement. Cross it off your list.

Now apply a second test to any measurement that has survived the above cut: The measurement must be compatible with all Three R's. For example, a measurement that encourages quick responsiveness to customers (the first R) may require the accumulation of excessive inventory (a violation of the third R). Drop it.

Whatever measurements survive that second cut are valid. Of course, if the survivors don't include cycle time, first-pass yield, cost, and productivity, add those. You now have a list of relevant measurements.

Can I change my own measurements?

Probably not officially, but who's stopping you from unofficially rating yourself by the above list? Start tracking your cycle time by using the simple formula of dividing actions in process by actions completed within a given period.

Tracking first-pass yield, which measures the quality of the business process you are responsible for, is a bit trickier, because people usually fail to identify and factor all the mistakes they correct during the process of completing a task. (There is a detailed discussion of this matter in my other book, *Getting Competitive.*) Those meaningful parameters, however, are exponential to the competitive mindset. They don't take long—probably five minutes each day—so it is practical to use them for your own information. Now at least *you* are monitoring the right things.

Have I really acquired the new, competitive mindset?

Only you know for sure. If, when you are assigned another task, you don't immediately think of what new resources you'll need to accomplish it, you have probably made the change. If you think in terms of simplifying a business process so you can get things done and *avoid* adding resources, that's another good sign. If you're beginning to feel lonely in a baseline environment, that's nature's way of telling you you're on your way.

How do I keep the new mindset alive?

If your company is moving toward entitlement, management will assume most of this responsibility. Part of the process is the installation of consistent, relevant, hierarchical measurements that get everybody thinking and talking the right way from top to bottom and let everybody see her or his role in the proper perspective.

If you're in a baseline company, keeping the mindset alive involves three little words: feedback, feedback, feedback. Spreading the word to peers and boss will of course also improve your stamina. And stick to your personal measurements!

What changes should I make if I get promoted?

Promotion is a distinct possibility if you follow the lessons of this book. When that occurs, you of course will be working with a bigger piece of the business process. The method of dealing with your new world, however, does not change. Look at the situation, search for non-value-added steps, start to reduce actions in process, root out substitute processes, and find ways to get rid of them. Put into place feedback loops on *all* processes so you can utilize Cycles of Learning. Since you're also directly responsible for improving the job satisfaction and security of people in your charge, be absolutely determined to spread your mindset to them. Then watch as Cycles of Learning do their work.

Empowerment: Seize It!

In truly competitive companies, the tacit empowerment of individuals at all levels is integral to survival. In such companies, the principle of self-empowerment is accepted and, when it gets results, rewarded.

A last reminder that self-empowerment involves saying no to work that adds no value. Even if you're not presently working in a competitive company, you surely recognize by now that barrier removal is a mission. Saying no and sharing your reasons with peers and boss takes gumption, to say the least. But if you know what you're talking about, you have a golden — and I mean golden — opportunity to start a ground swell in your immediate area. How far the ground swell spreads depends on how receptive (or desperate) your management is.

Ultimately, if your company is to survive, top brass must get the message. Meanwhile, however, your work life will become more meaningful and more interesting. Who knows, it could even get you a raise or promotion. Feeling better yet?

8

Your Personal Package

You *Can* Take It with You—
Total Cycle Time, That Is

Coming Full Circle

Earlier, I discussed how job security and satisfaction are inseparable and insisted that the way to find both is to locate yourself in a competitive professional environment. Also listed were the meaningful components of individual job security and satisfaction, everything from proper wages to fair treatment, showing that as a rule, your wants and those of your boss are very similar...in a competitive environment. Now that you are conversant with the techniques and values of Total Cycle Time, let's look again at your early want list in the light of your new knowledge.

To restate the case briefly:

- The good job you seek exists only in a competitive company.

- You have a key role to play in making your company competitive.

- A competitive company practices the Three R's.

- The Three R's are driven by the 5 I's of Total Cycle Time

Remember: Your approach to every aspect of your work—*subject matter*, *process*, and *culture*—should be retailored to

fit the goal of *adding value* and making your company competitive.

That is the situation in a nutshell. Now to review your individual want list in the language of Total Cycle Time.

Empowerment without Fear

Every employee and every manager wants to work in an environment that encourages spontaneity and initiative. Enlightened companies achieve that by empowering their people to
improve the business process, either by direct assignment to
cross-functional teams or through the unstructured process of
individual self-empowerment. Self-empowerment is gaining
converts daily. The concept is an inescapable element of competitiveness, because it helps to remove barriers. Individual empowerment extends the barrier removal process beyond the
limits of cross-functional teams and can thus be a very powerful
tool for improvement.

If you have (1) barrier removal skills, *consider yourself empowered. If you are not sure of a suspected barrier's nature, or
you feel you can't remove it, (2)* escalate the issue. *A cross-
functional team is probably called for.*

Getting Things Right the First Time

Everyone's job environment is enhanced when avoidable repetition, rework, and scrap become things of the past. Use the
feedback of Cycles of Learning to analyze a process, then improve your first-pass yield by applying your know-how. Make
that a habit and first-pass yield will cease to be a major headache. You *will* get things right the first time.

Focusing Your Energies on What Counts

If you have an inkling that you would accomplish more and achieve more recognition if there were fewer distractions, you are right. Barrier removal and cycle time reduction leave you with more time to think creatively because the daily interruptions and deliverables crises that haunt most working lives disappear.

Working within a Fair System

In business, a fair system is one that measures you on meaningful parameters: whether you are improving your company's responsiveness, accelerating results, and making the most of your resources. A fair system also requires you to work only on value-added steps.

Unless your company is already at entitlement, it may be up to you and your peers to start pushing objective criteria up the ladder of authority. The buck starts with you. Begin by applying the proper measurements to your own performance and spreading the mindset out to peers and managers. Get the boss involved. You can help create a fairer system, but you can't do it alone. Ultimately, your company's leaders must mobilize their best efforts to creating a consistent, objective system of measurements.

Fairness is a function of good leadership.

Security and Satisfaction through Superior Leadership

I've said it before, and I'll say it again: People are not the problem; processes are. Help clear away the obstructions to a seamless business process and your people problems will likewise diminish. Better leadership occurs naturally when your superiors apply a proper set of hierarchical measurements, shorten cycle times, exploit Cycles of Learning, and empower you to deal with them.

Better leadership inevitably follows when your superiors become educated in Total Cycle Time methods. Their performance will improve as the business process smoothes out. Their actions in process will decrease, and they, like you, can thus focus their energies on what counts. They will be out of the daily firefighting mode and into what really counts: adding value to seamless business processes. Many managers, even top managers, will jump at the chance to remove barriers once the rationale is clear.

Reality Check _____

Subject: Signetics
Source: John Macro, a Signetics manufacturing manager
Situation: The goals for Signetics were to drastically cut make/market cycle times, which were quite uncompetitive, and reverse a trend that threatened the company's future. The first step was to isolate the company's five manufacturing managers. This was done by removing them to our Louisiana facility and subjecting them to five days of intensive training. These were managers who for years had been plugging along, meeting frustration after frustration. Their morale and that of their employees was suffering. When told they were to be kingpins in a turnaround for Signetics, they were astounded—and delighted.

MACRO: No one had ever used that term before—a turnaround for Signetics. Then by the time we left, we were really very excited about what we could do to help Signetics.

Conclusion: Transformed and refocused within five days, those managers began Implementation immediately upon their return to the workplace.

MACRO: Before, we were not data-driven. We were just g[
with what we *thought* made sense. Now we're focused a[
have a concrete plan that will help us get very healthy ag[
The companywide work that is starting is exciting because
we sense now there is a real chance of making it.

At last, Macro and his peers were exhibiting confidence and
realizing substantial results.

Good leadership is a function of a competitive system.

Security and Satisfaction Through Higher-Quality Products

How much better will your company's products be once the
work force has eliminated non-value-added steps? How
much will the quality of those products improve when feedback is being systematically used to increase first-pass yield?
You know the answers.

Reality Check _____

Subject: B&B Electromatic

Situation: In 1988, B&B installed the monthly bonus award
system described in Chapter 2. Before that time, the
company's first-pass yield had been unacceptably low and the
scrap rate too high. As always, the preferred method for
correcting the problem was Cycles of Learning, but at B&B, the
bonus system further accelerated results because the connection
between better results and bigger bonuses was obvious to every
employee.

Outcome: Within a year, first-pass yield had increased to the
point that scrap was about zero and rework disappeared, a
condition that was reflected in monthly paychecks. Three years
later, productivity has tripled and quality has improved. Profit

is running 30 percent of sales, and inventory is at an all-time low — 12 percent of sales.

Everyone's job security increases when a company has a high-quality product line, as is the case with B&B. As is also the case with B&B, the quality of your company's products improves as cycle times are shortened and processes are simplified.

First-pass yield is the best measure of business process quality.

Adding steps to prevent defects defeats the purpose of a quality improvement program.

Security and Satisfaction through Quicker Response to Customers

Everyone's job security increases when your company can exploit windows of opportunity that suddenly open. Furthermore, customers are usually willing to pay a premium for quick, accurate, flexible response. Again, the post-turnaround B&B is a perfect example of the above premise.

Reality Check _____

Subject: B&B Electromatic

Situation: In 1989, the Canadian government solicited bids for a specially designed traffic barrier to control lane changes. The bidding deadline was so close that only B&B and one other company responded. But response time was more than a matter of quick bids; Canada wanted the products delivered in 3 months. The best the competition could do was 18. B&B won the contract and delivered the product a week ahead of the customer's request (so fast, in fact, that the surprised customer did not have funds available to pay the bill!).

Outcome: With that coup, a new niche of the traffic control business was penetrated and the way was cleared for substantial growth. Because it can usually develop new products in a quarter of the time required by competitors, B&B will certainly move into adjacent niches of its business.

In a time-based society, quick response is itself a salable product.

Improving Your Transferability

Promotions or Greener Pastures?

For many, job security turns on being promotable, and job security increases with every promotion. Suffice it to say that in a competitive company (or one that aspires to be competitive), a *mindset of barrier removal* with skills to match is about as good a promotion ticket as there is.

Another form of job security is the ability to take on any job you are asked to do within your operation, a quality I call *transferability*. When a company's productivity increases and its business processes get simpler, being versatile is a key factor in an individual's transferability. As you now know, the process of barrier removal is generic and adaptable to virtually every level of every business. If you master the competitive mindset and the art of spotting and dislodging barriers, and if you gain similar experience in using Cycles of Learning effectively, you will possess *generic, transferable skills* that can take you far beyond the subloop in which you currently work. Or beyond your present company!

In addition to promoting and implementing time-based management within the business community at large, we at Thomas Group also attempt to set ourselves up as a model for what we preach. Transferability is a perfect example. We hire specialists in one subject matter or another and teach them the principles and methods of Total Cycle Time. Once they have mastered those and have appropriate experience applying Total Cycle Time, partners can function effectively across the board: with smokestacks, silicon, software, hardware, aerospace, defense, services—you name it.

Generic business process barrier removal skills transcend subject matter expertise. These skills can be leveraged upward and outward.

Job Satisfaction and Total Cycle Time

Some elements of job satisfaction revolve around subject matter issues, personal chemistry, and individual taste. Most, however, do not. Many of the hangups blocking job satisfaction are generic issues that can be remedied.

Many of the personality problems that disrupt the workplace and threaten careers are aggravated by baseline conditions and would go away when those conditions change.

Seeing Is Believing: Making Work Meaningful

The low turnover in competitive, short-cycle-time companies demonstrates that people there are more satisfied with their jobs. A primary ingredient in this satisfaction is the regular feedback everyone receives, which shows them the results of their activities while such results are still hot. People are informed. They see clearly how their subloop contributes to the bigger picture. And by moving from baseline to entitlement, people have savored the satisfaction of empowerment. At entitlement, the defeatist mindset that links performance improvement to additional resources is totally discredited.

The question is no longer *if* performance can be improved but *how much* and *how soon.*

On-the-Job Variety

You can bet that once you've started the assault on barriers, your working life will involve enough change to make you sometimes long for the "not-so-good old days"! In addition, the ripple effect you create by spreading the word to peers and superiors represents a new and refreshing challenge.

At entitlement, you are freed from nagging, non-value-added distractions, which means that you can handle more and different tasks without extra effort or resources.

Knowing Where You Stand

As you have seen, the most effective way to know where you stand at work is to operate under a consistent, hierarchical set of measurements. By nature, hierarchical criteria fit into the next higher and lower levels of measurements, a pattern that is repeated from top to bottom. They give you precise assurance that your work is a constructive part of your company's process flow, and you have the added peace of mind of knowing that the measurements by which you are rated jibe with those at all other levels.

The Spin-off Effect: A New
Mindset for Your Private Life

A few pages back the word *transferability* was used to dramatize how your generic skill set allows you to perform effectively elsewhere in your company. But there is another kind of transferability that should interest you. Applying short-cycle-time values is a potent device for improving quality of life outside the workplace. Doing so becomes second nature once you've seen the results on the job.

The impact of the new mindset on your personal life can be detected in two ways. First, the mindset certainly makes off hours pleasanter. You will not arrive home from work worn down or discouraged by brick walls, concrete ceilings, or the other barriers that once sapped your energy. Second, your acquired know-how, if applied, makes your leisure time more satisfying because you use it more productively. There are at least as many barriers to smooth sailing at home as at work, and the same indices of improvement apply. If your at-home gain amounted to nothing more than a 25 percent time saving, think of what that would mean in terms of your options. For me, that's a lot of fishing! But of course the quality of your life will improve along with the time you save, and for the same reasons as at work.

Dallying Can Be Beautiful, Can't It?

An interesting side effect of short personal cycle times is what they reveal about your priorities and pleasures. For example, you may find when you remove all the barriers to effective shopping that something is missing—the relaxation of a stroll around a store and the aimless browsing that can be so pleasant. Likewise, after systematically determining the shortest, most efficient way to get to work, you may miss the scenic route. The point here is that in your leisure time, there may be some therapeutic value in *not* improving your productivity. The meter only runs at work.

However, everyone accepts without question a great many non-value-added steps in his or her personal life. I've already described my refusal to kill time in a doctor's office. But how many others would push for a more productive arrangement? Would you? Even if you're reluctant to adopt my solution of telephone consultations, you can at least call the doctor's office just before your scheduled appointment to find out how late the appointments are running (is it ever otherwise?) and react accordingly.

Until lately, a business acquaintance of mine was annoyed by a mounting wave of unsolicited telephone calls made to her home by people canvassing for charity, wishing to peddle some new long-distance phone deal, or whatever. These intrusions almost all occurred during the dinner hour (a practice that most people find particularly obnoxious). More important, they added no value to her leisure time.

At first, she distanced herself by installing an answering machine to do the dirty work, but sooner or later, she would have to listen to the entire message tape to glean the value-added calls from the rest. She was thus still victimized by non-value-adding intruders. Then she found a way around that barrier. She taped an answering machine greeting, using words to the following effect: "If you are soliciting, kindly hang up because I do not do business that way. If you are a friend or relative, please leave a message." Virtually all the unwanted intrusions evaporated, because a commercial caller has better uses of time than wasting it on a lost cause like that one.

The non-value-added steps outsiders inflict upon you are easier to spot than the ones you yourself perpetrate. For example, an acquaintance of mine decided to apply Total Cycle Time to his hobby, which is rustling up homemade pizzas for his family. Just for fun, he asked his wife to watch his very practiced operation and point out any steps she detected that added no value to the final product. He was astounded by the list she gave him. Although there was doubtless some fun in baking the old, inefficient way, eliminating those steps dramatically accelerated the pizza-making process.

Things Your Mother Told You

An amusing, inevitable result of applying personal cycle time techniques is the realization that to a small extent, they reaffirm some of the most irksome clichés of parental wisdom.

"Clean Up Your Room!"

Your parents were right about this, of course, as you probably discovered on your own long before you ever heard of Total Cycle Time. Getting adolescents to keep a tidy room is one of the biggest parental frustrations, and because tidiness is a touchy issue in the generation gap, young people have to learn the wisdom of the concept on their own.

The teenage daughter of a friend made sloppiness a symbol of her independence until she realized she was spending ungodly amounts of time tracking down items that had disappeared into the midden pile she called her "space." That realization prompted a major turnaround. Now it's Mom who is lectured on the virtues of neatness.

"Neatness Counts!"

It counts more than many people realize. When it comes to quality of life, neatness often counts more than overzealous "cleanliness." A clinically sanitary, eat-off-the-floor room can be oppressive if it isn't neat. However, few people object to a little dust here and there if things are shipshape.

Reality Check _____

Subject: Charlie Burden

Situation: Charlie Burden is a manic collector with a houseful of dust catchers that defied his good housekeeping instincts. For Charlie, the thrill is the pursuit of collectibles, not their care and feeding. Things got to the point that dusting and vacuuming preempted weekends once spent on the antiques trail before he realized that he could cut house cleaning by two-thirds if he simply kept his digs tidy.

Outcome

BURDEN: Once everything was in its place, my house looked
spotless whether or not I had dusted in the last week or so.
And after I'd gotten my collections carefully arranged, they
looked better and didn't get underfoot—or very dirty! Now

I devote most of my old vacuum-and-mop time to visiting flea markets!

"A Sound Mind in a Healthy Body"

There is no question that regular exercise equips you to make the most of your potential on and off the job. Puzzling, however, are those people who clearly hate to exercise yet sweat their way through a strenuous daily regimen. According to medical consensus, exercising three times a week is enough to keep a person fit. Why, then, (unless it is sheer pleasure or fulfills another important objective) engage in non-value-added endeavor on the other four days? It's your time.

"You'd Better Write That Down!"

Here is another cliché that more often than not is ignored. What sort of vanity prompts people to trust too often to memory? The fact is that however versatile your brain may be, you are creating unnecessary, distractive mental clutter by trying to keep a headful of schedules and trivia. And when the inevitable time arrives that one's memory really isn't what it used to be, there is no excuse whatever for avoiding paper and pencil. If you've ever emerged from the supermarket checkout with a cartful of groceries only to realize that you'd forgotten that tube of toothpaste you meant to buy, you know how little value there is in a second trip through the checkout line.

Reality Check _____

Subject: Barbara Atwood
Situation: Selective written reminders also save forgetful embarrassments. Every January, while the post-Christmas sales are on, Barbara Atwood buys a pocket datebook and immediately notes in it every holiday and family birthday for the entire year. She also buys in one transaction all the greeting cards and valentines she expects to send, along with extras for her kids.

Conclusion: In one fell swoop, she has eliminated the possibility of overlooking dear old Aunt Minnie and she has saved herself a year's worth of a la carte trips to Ye Olde Gift Shoppe. Barbara figures she's freed up at least two days a year through that single, simple process.

"Practice Makes Perfect!"

Or in the language of Total Cycle Time, "Cycles of Learning accelerate results" — if you use feedback properly!

Why is it that trimming a Christmas tree is always a complicated process with a cycle time that has to be seen to be believed? It's because the Cycles of Learning are too few and far between. Why is it that when I type on my terminal, it takes me at least twice as long to finish as when one of the secretaries is in charge? Again, it's because I've had fewer Cycles of Learning. However, when my wife Wayne and I pack for a vacation, I'm the one with the edge. Countless business trips have cut my packing time to about a quarter of the time Wayne needs.

Reality Check _____

Subject: Debbie Barber
Solution: Early last year, I hired Debbie as executive assistant. I quickly noticed that she carried about three times as much luggage as I did on the same trip. Several Cycles of Learning later, she had cut her freight requirements by two-thirds without any visible sacrifice. The trick, of course, is to make those cycles work for you in every part of your personal life that you would like to streamline.

"The Early Bird Gets the Worm"

Not necessarily. Recently, in a Sunday supplement magazine, there was one of those quick, ten-question tests that pop up so often. This one promised to determine whether the taker appreciated the value of time. One question was, "Do you arrive a half-hour early for work or an appointment?" The "correct" answer was yes, presumably because anyone serious

about time can't afford to be late. My answer was "incorrec
of course. Who has a half hour to kill waiting for activities
begin as scheduled? There are plenty of better uses for half
an hour—provided, of course, that you are always on time.

Homelife: How Systematic Can You Get?

You can get as systematic at home as you are in the workplace.
The same methods can be brought to bear to help you use free
time more satisfactorily, although the absence of precise data
will require you to do more guesswork. As always, the components are cycle time, first-pass yield, and value added.

Reality Check _____

Subject: Bonnie Sloan, TGI partner
Solution: During the cycle time reduction project at
Coleman, mentioned earlier, Bonnie Sloan suddenly found
herself in a tight spot, time-wise.

As she recalls, "I had a scheduled meeting with a company
owner and board member and only had clothes suitable for
factory wear with me in Wichita. In order to make the right
impression at the meeting, I felt I needed the right business suit.
[But] sharing a car with the team, I had only one hour to shop."

Because Bonnie usually sees shopping as leisurely recreation,
she feared that she might find herself arriving late to the
meeting or looking disrespectfully underdressed. So she
reviewed the business process required to purchase a suitable
wardrobe. Experience told her that her baseline for such a task
had been as long as a day. Her first-pass yield at baseline was
less than perfect because she liked to mull things over instead
of making quick decisions, and she was not always able to find
everything she needed in one trip.

In this case, Bonnie knew exactly what she had to do and
how long she had to do it, so her entitlement was a given:

"My shopping entitlement was a one-hour cycle time and a
well-fitting, professional-looking wool suit, conservative blouse,

medium heels, and a matching purse, all of which had to meet budgetary requirements. I mentally reviewed the known barriers:

- I enjoy window shopping and rarely stay focused.
- I enjoy clothes and often try numerous styles and outfits before making a decision.
- Petite sizes are difficult to find.
- I have a hard time focusing myself to pay some of today's high prices."

Outcome: Bonnie's list isolated the non-value-added steps. She subtracted the required time for those and preselected a local mall with all the requisite stores in one place. Then she made her move. She had hit entitlement on the nose and therefore did not have to rush to accomplish her task. In fact, she was able to make all the purchases with time to spare.

Bonnie thus was able to attend that important meeting on comfortable terms. Meanwhile, she had learned something about the use of personal time: "I realized my past shopping trips rarely stayed focused and had no cycle time goal. Since then, I have indeed institutionalized short-cycle-time shopping. Even errand running is now carefully orchestrated, because I am usually under time constraints. I must admit, however, that time permitting, I still enjoy a leisurely stroll through the mall, looking, tasting, touching, and trying on!"

Reality Check

Subject: Housing—to Rent or to Buy?
Source: Bonnie Sloan
Situation: Bonnie has since applied Total Cycle Time techniques to other personal matters. For example, she had to decide whether to buy or rent a dwelling in the Dallas area: "The process I used in the buy-versus-rent analysis I also used for defining my personal financial goals (investment objectives and strategies, both long- and short-term). I believe it will work well in any major decision-making circumstance. Once you get past your personal culture barriers (such as emotional responses, instinctive biases, and insecurities) and put pen to paper, real problem solving begins. Getting past cultural

barriers means letting the objective criteria do the talking and deciding accordingly.

"The initial step in overcoming the rent-or-buy problem is internal brainstorming, soul-searching with your mind. "It's an intellectual exercise, and an individual (versus a group) activity. First, I had to brainstorm the scope of the task and the *best approach to barrier removal*. I decided to make a chart and clarify my main objectives, and then set my 'entitlements.'

"The main *objectives* were to provide myself with the security of a comfortable, safe, enjoyable, affordable lifestyle. The *entitlements* were:

- Value (for cost or monthly payment)
- Affordability
- Time preservation (no long commutes)
- Safety
- Comfort
- Sociability.

"Then, I listed steps or subprocesses required to reach each entitlement:

- Rent or monthly payment (at or below $X per month)
- Low maintenance
- Good location (near airport, office, and shopping)
- A safe community (alarm or police protection)
- Landscaping
- Low traffic
- Quiet
- Recreational opportunities
- Mixed-age population (some singles).

"I began listing barriers and then brainstormed solutions. Some of the barriers were:

- Down payments
- Depreciation versus appreciation
- Commitment
- Tax considerations
- Lifestyle."

Outcome: "The solution brainstorming session reviewed all the apartments and housing options that I explored. Each were categorized by:

- Financial impact
- Existing barriers
- Effects on entitlements.

"I defined an *action plan*, which turned out to be a decision to buy a townhouse. It is in a suburb near the airport, with a neighborhood pool, private canal, walkways, landscaping, and a security patrol. I have been there six months and am very pleased with my *buy* decision!"

A question as big as that one can keep you stewing indefinitely if you let "feelings" – the emotional reactions to making a major, costly, possibly risky decision – have the upper hand. Or you can do what Bonnie did and save time. Bonnie's process meets the criteria for any cycle time approach. It was responsive to needs, it accelerated results, and it maximized the effectiveness of her existing resources. Furthermore, it provided an objective problem-solving framework to overcome emotional qualms. Sound too detached? Maybe. But consider the rewards of getting the decision made.

Brainstorming Outside the Workplace

Because Bonnie Sloan was a household unit of one, her brainstorming process was unilateral. If, however, your spouse or other family members are involved, you can organize them as you would a cross-functional team and set up brainstorming sessions as described in Chapter 7. Family members might surprise themselves with their creativity if you offer a small reward incentive for every idea or suggestion they provide, regardless of quality.

The potential of cross-functional brainstorming doesn't stop with household organization. It can apply to smooth out the processes within athletic teams, fitness clubs, hobby clubs, country clubs, scout troops, condo boards, historical societies, or civic groups. Organizations like these traditionally suffer from sluggish decision making and unproductive processes that perpetuate problems and discourage would-be members.

Reality Check _____

Subject: Sue Christensen, Zytec Corporation, Redwood Falls, Minnesota

Situation: At Zytec, Sue Christensen was exposed to brainstorming during a cycle time program that slashed her company's total cycle time from 80 to 5 days. Impressed by the "family atmosphere" the technique created, she adapted it for problem solving at her local church.

CHRISTENSEN: There are specific rules, like no idea is stupid, no criticizing or talking during someone else's turn, and money is no object [when thinking up a suggestion].

Outcome: The result has been creative solutions to problems and the involvement of new people in the church's problem-solving activities.

Once you've seen how using the cross-functional brainstorming approach improves any organization, what's to stop you from designing a Total Cycle Time project for your favorite organization? (But be careful; they'll probably want to elect you president.)

Your Personal Piece of the Big Picture

Your job security and satisfaction have an importance far beyond helping you achieve the time of your life, because a rewarding job situation is indicative of a competitive company, which in turn is indicative of the nation's competitive standing. Doing right by yourself is, therefore, far from self-centered. It can, in fact, make a positive, measurable impact upon the United States' critical struggle for competitiveness.

Overcoming the "Little Me" Syndrome

General Bullmoose, the capitalist tycoon who used to appear in Al Capp's *Li'l Abner* comic strip, was fond of declaiming, "What's good for General Bullmoose is good for the country!" That famous remark, a satirical approximation of the expressed mindset of GM's top management, was meant to convey the hidebound egomania of captains of U.S. industry. But that was then; this is now. Today, if General Bullmoose's company operated at entitlement, the statement would be absolutely on the mark. Corporate competitiveness benefits everyone, from General Bullmoose to yourself.

With that in mind, consider how important competitive mindset is beyond the personal benefits it is apt to bring you. This concept is sometimes difficult to appreciate, especially among people who work at the low end of the corporate totem pole, among whom a common attitude is: "What difference does it make what I do except to me?" The answer is *plenty*.

When you adopt the new mindset, you must understand that no matter where you are in the company hierarchy, the impact of your work ripples to the very top of your organization. Remember the barrier circle effect. At baseline, the process barriers that bug you also bug the performance of the subloop with which you connect. That subloop's performance in turn impacts the overall loop, which is just one step away from your CEO. So the impact of your contribution in barrier removal is companywide, not local. To paraphrase the General: In a move to entitlement, what's good for you is good for your company.

Now you must look beyond the boundaries of your company's well-being. For your industry to survive in today's world, all the players will have to get competitive or, metaphor-ically speaking, die. How they fare will determine the quality of life in the United States for years to come, and U.S. businesses of all types are faced by a formidable array of Pacific Rim and European competitors who are diversifying at an alarming rate.

Meanwhile, the nation's economic health depends upon re-versing the alarming trade deficit. Otherwise, our accus-tomed standard of living will decline further. To lick the trade deficit, we must overtake and outperform foreign com-petitors by offering products with higher quality and more attractive features in less time than it takes them to do so.

How? By applying Total Cycle Time concepts in every nook and cranny of U.S. industry and U.S. institutions. By recogniz-ing that competitiveness is a function of *responsiveness*, acceler-ating *results*, and effective use of *resources* — the Three R's — all of which are driven by time. Consider for a moment which parts of the United States will become economically strong. The future belongs to those states that offer rapid response to changing economic times, places where the traditional, non-value-added bureaucratic red tape has been supplanted by an enlightened, responsive policy that welcomes businesses and people who are competitive on today's terms.

Beyond the United States, the future belongs to the na-tions whose companies are quick at responding to economic opportunity — fast countries. Fast countries will be the ones with better communications, better infrastructure, better public services, and better technological innovation. Fast countries will be the ones whose industries have shortened cycle times, use the lessons of experience to advantage, and do things right the first time.

In tomorrow's world, the big will not outperform the small. The fast will outperform the slow.

To paraphrase old General Bullmoose one more time: What's good for you and your company is good for the coun-try. Whether the United States wins the time war and becomes a fast country depends on the competitiveness of its component economic parts: companies that win the battle for entitlement and time warriors like yourself.

You are empowered.

You can win.

The decision is yours.

Index

About the Author

Philip R. Thomas is founder and chairman of Thomas Group, Inc., an Irving, Texas-based business turnaround firm. His Total Cycle Time ^{SM} system is the result of 20 years' work at Texas Instruments, General Instrument, Fairchild, and RCA. Since 1978, he has successfully introduced Total Cycle Time-based management to improve corporate competitiveness and streamline operational and new product cycle times at companies ranging from Fortune 10 firms to entrepreneurial start-ups, from the aerospace industry to financial services. He is also the author of *Competitiveness Through Total Cycle Time: An Overview for CEOs* and *Getting Competitive: Middle Managers and the Cycle Time Ethic*, which show how to plan and successfully implement TCT strategies in any kind of company.

This book was written with **Kenneth R. Martin**, a specialist in business and maritime history. In addition to three book projects with Philip R. Thomas, Martin is the author, coauthor, or editor of a dozen books and more than fifty articles on a wide range of subjects, including a company history of Thomas Group, Inc. He lives in Woolwich, Maine.